SNOBOL
An Introduction to Programming

Hayden Computer Programming Series

James N. Haag, Consulting Editor
Professor of Computer Science and Physics
University of San Francisco

SNOBOL
An Introduction to Programming

Peter R. Newsted
School of Business Administration
University of Wisconsin—Milwaukee

HAYDEN BOOK COMPANY, INC.
Rochelle Park, New Jersey

Library of Congress Cataloging in Publication Data

Newsted, Peter R
   SNOBOL : an introduction to programming

   (Hayden computer programming series)
   Includes index.
   1. SNOBOL (Computer program language). I. Title.
QA76.73.S6N48   001.6'425   74-30428
ISBN 0-8104-5782-2

1   2   3   4   5   6   7   8   9   PRINTING

75 76 77 78 79 80 81 82   YEAR

Preface

SNOBOL (StriNg Oriented symBOlic Language) does not put a premium on mathematical skills when a person uses it to communicate with a computer. It is not a mysterious language or one that threatens or intimidates. It is a powerful programming tool that can be used with minimal knowledge of computer architecture and jargon. Thus SNOBOL has a much wider use than its string and symbol orientation suggests. Tasks ranging from understanding English sentences to maintaining business records have been successfully programmed in SNOBOL.*

"SNOBOL: An Introduction to Programming" is intended as a beginner's text in SNOBOL; it can easily be used for a first course in programming--as an alternative to FORTRAN. Without stumbling over complexities which have been relegated to appendices, novices can gain a mastery of SNOBOL which will allow them to perform many powerful string and symbol manipulation tasks.

This book can be viewed as a companion or introduction to a complete description of SNOBOL. In classroom testing and development of this book, I have found this combination approach quite

---

*For those interested in full-scale production work, two different compilers exist for SNOBOL. SPITBOL is available for IBM hardware; FASBOL runs on UNIVAC equipment. With these compilers, programs run at least five to ten times faster than under the SNOBOL interpreter on the same machine.

successful. Students are given a simple introduction, but still have the complete documentation and description available when they need it.

The following three-step method has worked well in practice. First, a selection of exercises is completed as the language is being taught. After this basic mastery of the language, the sample program in Appendix 4 is discussed to point out additional features of the language. Finally, students are ready to attempt a project on their own--ideally in their own discipline or area of interest.

As exercises are started, students also find it useful to glance ahead to Chapter 8 which lists common errors. Having a feeling for such mistakes may reduce, though certainly not eliminate, their occurrence.

Peter R. Newsted

Milwaukee, Wisconsin

Contents

Chapter 1.
What Is a Computer
(And How Does SNOBOL Fit In)

>>> A Computer Is Like Everyday Life

A computer is a highly demanding but very useful servant. The
fact that it is a servant and not a master should not be forgotten, for those who believe it is a master are easily intimidated
and fail to use it to its fullest. This intimidation can be
avoided through knowledge.

As a first step to this knowledge consider the following analogy between a computer system and a fictitious business office.
The boss in the office (Mr. Riggsby) dictates a memo for a secre-
tary (Ms. Kingsley) to have typed and distributed. Ms. Kingsley,
who supervises the typing pool, may never have met Riggsby and
really knows him only through his dictation tapes. When she
receives a tape, she first listens to it to hear any special
instructions such as deadlines, kind of paper, or other information she must get. Once it is determined that 50 mimeographed
copies are needed and should incorporate company guidelines on sex
discrimination with a prefacing message from Mr. Riggsby, she is
ready to begin.

As the memo is a simple task she delegates it to Howard who is

1

the office boy for the typing pool. Howard gets mimeo masters,
sits down at a typewriter and types Mr. Riggsby´s message followed
by the discrimination guidelines. He then runs off copies and
distributes them.

   A computer system is quite similar to this. A programmer, a
program, a central processing unit, a computer language, a supervisory monitor, a memory, hardware and software, source code and
object code, input and output are all to be seen here. Mr.
Riggsby is the programmer; he issues instructions on his special
dictation tape. This input is a program to be executed by the
computer. The computer in this case is the typing pool. Ms.
Kingsley is the supervisory or monitor program of the computer,
for it is she who sets in motion the preparation of the memo.
Such a job scheduler gives tasks to compilers, in this case
Howard, who translate them to a form a machine (be it a mimeograph
or a computer) can actually use. Howard carries out his task
based on Ms. Kingsley´s instructions. The masters he prepares
can be viewed as memory in the computer; this is where information
is stored for further processing (which in this case will lead to
output). The physical machines being used are called hardware.
The dictating machine (used for input to the typing pool) is like
a keypunch or a teletypewriter, the typewriter--a central
processing unit (CPU) capable of many different actions, and the
mimeograph--an output printer.

   The sets of instructions used here are programs or software.
Riggsby gave his initial terse instructions (the job control
language) and his message (the source code) to Kingsley. She

noted the system requirements (i.e. that compiler Howard was necessary to process Riggsby's message) and called Howard to set them in motion. Howard concisely deciphered and edited Riggsby's rambling message to a form (object code) he could use on his typewriter and then have printed via the mimeograph machine.

This analogy (or folk tale as it has become) has one final point. If the programmer (Mr. Riggsby) is to continue to be successful he must not be intimidated by the computer system (Ms. Kingsley, Howard, and their machines), for if he is all is lost.

>>> If It Is Like Everyday Life, Why Is It Confusing?

There are several things characteristic of computers and the programs they execute which apparently make them both mysterious and incomprehensible to the novice. Speed and accuracy are easy to accept. Machines always seem to have these. A memory is new. How can a machine "remember" instructions and data that it is given? Most types of machines don't remember anything.

A COMPUTER'S MEMORY. Storing information in a computer is really quite simple. Fundamentally it is no different from the way a tape recorder "remembers" words or music. Information is encoded magnetically, just as is sound.* Each letter, number, or special symbol which can be entered on a punch card at a keypunch or typed in at a teletypewriter is represented by a different

---

*Newer memories use more sophisticated electronic techniques, but the effect is the same.

magnetic code. The real memory of a computer is composed of
millions--even billions--of very tiny magnets. Each magnet can be
magnetized in one of two ways: to represent either the digit
"zero" or the digit "one". When a magnet is in one of these
states, it is referred to as a bit (of information). Groupings of
eight or so of these bits represent a given letter, number, or
symbol. A group of this kind is called a byte. If the byte of a
given computer does contain eight bits, it can be magnetized in
256 ways (2 x 2 x 2 x 2 x 2 x 2 x 2 x 2 = 256) and hence can
represent any one of 256 possible characters. With this many
possibilities all the letters of the alphabet (lower as well as
upper case), the 10 digits, and many special characters (e.g. *,
/, ?, =, +) can be easily represented in a computer's memory.

A combination of four or more bytes makes up a typical computer
word. And it is this word which is the basic unit of computer
memory. Large computers customarily have several hundred thousand
such words of memory storage.

A COMPUTER'S BEHAVIOR. The other difficult thing to conceive
about a computer is that it apparently "behaves"--frequently in an
all too human fashion. A computer does this only because it has
been programmed to do so. It is really this program which must be
considered in explaining a computer's behavior.

Instructions to a computer (the program it runs) can be given
in many different languages. Some languages seem very obscure and
bear a close resemblance to the zero and one structure of a
computer's memory. Others are mathematically based. Still

others--such as SNOBOL--come closer to English and are therefore comparatively easy to use with no prior experience with computers.

>>> What It Means To Write a SNOBOL Program

COMMUNICATING WITH A COMPUTER. Instructions to a computer are in the form of a program. Ideas are expressed or "programmed" in the coded format of a computer language such as SNOBOL. The result is a program which the computer can execute.

A computer accepts this code from 80 column punch cards that have been prepared on a keypunch or from a file in the computer's memory which contains card "images" that have been entered from a teletypewriter terminal connected to the computer.

Typically, a prospective user of SNOBOL should master the use of a keypunch or teletypewriter with a very simple, instructor-supplied program so that any real programming problems encountered will not be compounded by difficulties with these machines.

PROGRAMMING AND "VARIABLES". A computer language like SNOBOL allows the user to specify the computer's actions. By means of a language, a computer can be told to process a computer word or group of computer words. A computer word grouping or variable (so called because its contents can vary) is the fundamental part of a computer language. It has special features in SNOBOL. It is easily thought of as a box which has a name and can contain any number of characters. For example the following SNOBOL statement

sets up a variable called PIE which accepts and temporarily contains the literal string of characters B-L-A-C-K-B-I-R-D.

$$PIE = \text{'BLACKBIRD'}$$

FLOW OF CONTROL. The sequence of actions indicated by the
program is called the flow of control. Flow of control in programming can be likened to following a recipe. Consider the
following:

BLACKBIRD PIE

2 cups flour

1/3 cup water

2/3 cups shortening

1 teaspoon salt

4 blackbirds

20 blackbirds

Combine half of the first four ingredients to make a
bottom crust. Make this crust by adding the ingredients in
small amounts mixing slightly until a dough is obtained. Roll
out with a rolling pin using extra flour to keep dough from
sticking.*

Combine the remainder of the first four ingredients to
make a top crust. Follow the same directions used for the
bottom crust.

---

*Those who quibble with these directions are well on their way to
understanding that some programs can do a given task better than
others.

Place bottom crust in a pie pan.

Subdue blackbirds and place in the pie pan.

Put on top crust to restrain belligerent blackbirds.

Bake until crust is done.

Set before the King.

The recipe is the program and the person following the instructions is the computer. Ideally the person will do exactly what the recipe directs--using certain conventions in case of ambiguity. For example, if all of the ingredients are listed with no mixing instructions, one would add them in order until the last one had been used. The same holds for a series of statements in a computer program; they are executed by the computer sequentially unless there are instructions to the contrary. With the pie recipe such contrary instructions are, "Combine HALF of the first four ingredients to make a bottom crust". The first four ingredients are processed a SECOND time before the last two are considered. Implicit in these instructions is that the pie maker can count and thus determine the first, second, third, and fourth ingredients on the recipe card. In other words, "first", "second" etc. are (implicit) LABELS which tell which things to use.

The recipe analogy has one more point which is useful in explaining flow of control. There are explicit references in the recipe to GO TO other parts of the recipe. For example, "Follow the same directions used for the bottom crust," tells the pie maker to go back to the previous instructions and repeat them for

making the top crust. The same thing is frequently required in a
program. One part of the program may transfer control to another
part of the program, thereby interrupting the sequential flow of
control.

Hence the instructions which the computer has been given in the
form of SNOBOL code guide the processing it is to do, just as
English "code" has been used to give the recipe for Blackbird Pie.
To make this guidance more flexible, parts of the program which
will be referred to must have name tags or labels; further, other
parts of the code must have provisions to refer or go to these
parts. How this is done in SNOBOL will be seen in the following
chapters. Without labels or gotos, instructions are executed in
sequence without any possibility of repeating a given set.

WHAT MAKES SNOBOL UNIQUE. Using any computer language, it is
possible to do repetitive processing and checking of variables
(frequently using arithmetic). What makes SNOBOL special is that
its variables can hold virtually endless strings of characters
(formed from numbers, letters, special symbols, or blanks).
SNOBOL variables are often called "string variables" because of
this capability. SNOBOL variables are said to have a "null" value
when they are empty and thus store nothing. As blanks are legitimate characters, a variable which contains one or more blanks is
NOT empty and therefore not null.

The SNOBOL language allows the building up and the modification
of the contents of these string variables, the processing of their
contents in terms of checking for certain real words or symbols

and replacing, deleting or adding other real words or symbols.
For instance in SNOBOL a user can say if VIEW contains CRESTED &
RED WING SPOTS or CRESTED & BUFF-COLORED BODY store CEDAR WAXWING
in CHECK.LIST. The following code actually accomplishes this:

```
   VIEW ´CRESTED´ (´RED WING SPOTS´ | ´BUFF-COLORED BODY´) :F(END)
STORE CHECK.LIST = ´CEDAR WAXWING´
END
```

This kind of alternative pattern matching is SNOBOL´s strength.
Pattern matching facilities in SNOBOL permit a user to specify
virtually any pattern he can conceive of and then interrogate any
variable to see if the pattern matches or is contained in the
variable. Any sequence of symbols can be matched. Further, such
a match can be made to depend on the prior or additional occurrence of other symbols.

>>> Areas of SNOBOL Application

   SNOBOL is not just for bird watchers, however.

   LINGUISTIC APPLICATIONS. SNOBOL programs can handle many types
of linguistic tasks. For example a concordance for a text could
be generated. Such a task would involve the indexing of all words
in the text and noting the frequency and context of their occurrence.*

---

*A variety of this kind of program was used to generate the index
 for this book.

More complex linguistic analysis is also possible. In translation and parsing where context is all important, SNOBOL can aid in
the extracting of contextual patterns. Winograd, for example, has
used SNOBOL to construct a system which can answer English language questions about the positions of objects in three dimen-
sional space.*

SNOBOL has also been used to analyze interview profiles and
textual passages to detect the presence of traits and concepts
ranging from agressiveness to judicial orientation.

SIMULATION APPLICATIONS. Behavior and process modeling or
simulation is possible in SNOBOL. A model of behavior could be
constructed as a SNOBOL program. Such a model, if correct, would
be expected to respond to stimuli the same way an actual person
does. The advantage of using a computer language to phrase a
theory is that nothing is ambiguous in the theory. Everything
must be precise if the computer is to work with it. Further,
unexpected consequences of complexly related assumptions can be
uncovered.

For example, a psychologist might be interested in a person's
learning a long list of words--seeing each word only once. It
would probably occur to the psychologist that previous familiarity
with the words would influence learning. He might postulate that
there is a greater possibility that the more familiar words would
be learned and therefore later remembered. This sounds very

*Winograd, T. UNDERSTANDING NATURAL LANGUAGE, Academic Press, New
 York, 1972.

respectable, but the psychologist has not defined what he means by
"familiarity" and "memory" or even "learning" and "recall".

To phrase a theory like this as a computer simulation, memory
could be viewed simply as a long list. Familiarity might mean
that familiar words have multiple occurrences on this list.
Learning would be a marking of familiar words (e.g. with a special
character such as a prime sign) and adding unfamiliar words at the
end of the list. Obviously, familiar words would be found first
during recall (if the list was searched from the beginning). This
simulation would also predict that as the search became less
limited (e.g. more time was allowed), some of the unfamiliar words
might be recalled--particularly those first encountered.

Probably, the resulting theory will be readily criticized as it
is made clearer by means of a simulation, for the best theory is
the one which can be easily disproved. Clearly it is easier to
disprove transparent theories than ambiguous ones. For example,
this sample learning theory might be criticized because it says
memory is organized in a linear and not a hierarchical fashion.
But the point is memory IS organized by the theorist. Therefore,
by using theories phrased as computer simulations in a language
such as SNOBOL better theories can hopefully result.

GAMES USING SNOBOL. Almost any kind of game can be programmed
in SNOBOL. SNOBOL programs have been written to play bridge, tic
tac toe, hangman, gin rummy, even football. The string variables
in SNOBOL are quite useful for defining both the strategy and the
mechanics of a game.

COMPILERS CAN BE WRITTEN IN SNOBOL. With SNOBOL's ability to
match patterns and move them around, it is a natural tool of the
computer scientist who wants to write a program or "compiler" to
translate one computer language into another. Though SNOBOL is
not efficient enough to be used for everyday compilers, it can be
quite useful in setting up experimental versions. For example, a
SNOBOL program exists which converts programs written in the
FORTRAN computer language to the BASIC computer language.

ADDITIONAL POSSIBILITIES. Table 1-1 gives a list of other
applications which have been attempted in SNOBOL. All of these
applications are possible in other computer languages. Their
users have chosen SNOBOL because they found their task simpler in
this language. Just as it is easier to express things in one
foreign language (or English) rather than another, so it is true
with computer languages; any task a computer can do can be written
in almost any computer language. It is no more than a question of
clarity, number of instructions, and time.

TABLE 1-1.   SNOBOL Uses.

The following listing in revised form from the "SNOBOL4 Newslet-
ter" (Published at Bell Telephone Laboratories, Holmdel, New
Jersey, March 1, 1969) indicates actual uses to which SNOBOL has
been put. These applications are in the words of the users themselves, and hence indicate both general and specific uses.

COMPUTER SCIENCE

instruction in computer science
macro processing
translation of programming languages
computer-assisted instruction
information retrieval
experimental compilers
translation of FORTRAN source code
FORTRAN macro generator
generation of FORTRAN cross-
    reference tables
resequencing of FORTRAN programs
preprocessing of FORTRAN programs
language interpreters
source language modification
program conversion
file manipulation
compiler writing
programming research
programming language experimentation
heuristic programming
source deck processing
code generation
systems programming development
language development
metacompilers

PSYCHOLOGY

psychological simulation
modeling psychological processes
simulation of concept learning

LINGUISTICS

syntactic analysis
grammar testing
text analysis
natural language processing
concordances
parsing algorithms
transformational grammar
    testing
phonological rule testing
text processing
text searching
syntactic transformation
content analysis

GENERAL

symbolic algebra
    manipulations
encoding English into
    Braille
artificial intelligence
    research
text editing
automatic indexing
list processing
data shaping
text formatting
simulation
pattern recognition
information structure
    processing
data laundry
cryptanalysis
symbol manipulation

THE ARTS   GENERAL (continued)

stylistic analysis   compilation of
literary research   bibliographies
music analysis   medical history taking
graphic arts   engineering applications
music synthesis   symbolic mathematics
                                  nonnumeric data structures
                                  information science
BUSINESS   theorem proving
                                  logic
management information systems

EXERCISES

1. Find the input/output site or sites for your computer center.
Are they adjacent to the computer's CPU?

2. Learn how to use a keypunch and/or a teletypewriter if you
don't already know.

3. Construct a diagram which captures the relationships of such
terms as keypunch, teletypewriter, CPU, memory, printer, hardware,
software, program, compiler, and other relevant components of
computer use. Draw upon both what has been described in this
chapter and what has been said in class discussion.

4. Describe a problem in your own discipline or area of interest
which might be aided by the use of SNOBOL and its emphasis on
patterns and real words rather than numbers.

Chapter 2.
The 3 Basic SNOBOL Statements

There are three basic types of instructions or ways of saying things in SNOBOL. The general format of each type is described here; more examples are given later.

THE ASSIGN STATEMENT. This statement stores characters or other symbols into a variable. One or more such things can be stored into a variable with a single assign statement:*

```
GENERAL FORMAT:  variable ^ = ^ object(s)
RESULTING ACTION:  Variable now contains object(s).
```

PIE = ´APPLES & SUGAR´ is an actual assign statement which stores the 14 literal characters which are enclosed in single quotes as the contents of the variable named PIE.

---

*Lower case letters are used in these and succeeding examples to indicate variables or contents in general; they would be replaced by a specific variable name or literal in an actual statement. One or more spaces is necessary wherever a "^" is used in these initial brief descriptions.

THE MATCH STATEMENT. Here an object is inspected to see if it
contains another specific object or series of such objects. The
computer can be instructed to take action based on the success or
failure of the match (i.e. the flow of control can be modified):

```
GENERAL FORMAT:  object(s).1 ^ object(s).2
RESULTING ACTION:  Object(s).1 is inspected for object(s).2.
```

A match statement like PIE ´CHERRIES´ thus asks if the
variable PIE contains the eight consecutive letters enclosed in
quotes.

THE MATCH AND REPLACE STATEMENT. This is a combination of the
assign and match statements. Here an object is examined to see if
it contains something and if it does it is replaced with something
else. Unmatched contents of the variable are not altered:

```
GENERAL FORMAT:  object(s).1 ^ object(s).2 ^ = ^ object(s).3
RESULTING ACTION:  If object(s).2 is found in object(s).1 it is
                   replaced with object(s).3.
```

For example, the match and replace statement:

        SPOON ´SUGAR´ = ´SALT´

tries to find five consecutive letters which spell sugar, and if a
match for these letters is found in SPOON, then these letters are
replaced with letters which spell salt.

>>> Literals vs. Variables

   Before proceeding to more examples of these three statements,
it is helpful to have in mind a clear distinction between literals
and variables. Variables have already been described as boxes
with names (e.g. PIE and SPOON). Such boxes can have varying
contents and thus they are called variables. These
contents--which can be letters, numbers, and other symbols--are
referred to by mentioning the NAME of the variable which holds
them.
   There is another important way to refer to characters and
symbols, however. They can be mentioned directly by enclosing
them in quotes (either single (´) or double(")). When this is
done, the string of characters and symbols and their surrounding
quote marks are called a literal (e.g. ´APPLE´, ´CHERRIES´,
´SUGAR´, and ´SALT´). Variables AND literals can be used wherever
"object(s)" is used in the three kinds of SNOBOL statements just
described. This usage should become clearer in the examples which
follow.

>>> Examples of the 3 Basic SNOBOL Statements

   ASSIGN STATEMENTS. The following four lines are SNOBOL assign
statements:

```
        CAGE.1 =  ´TIGER´
        CAGE.2 =    "BEAR"
```

```
CAGE.3 =            ´ZEBRA´
CRATE        =      "POLAR BEAR"
```

Figure 2-1 has a pictorial representation of these statements. The shape around the contents is an arbitrary one selected for clarity.   A rectangle or other shape could be used instead.

FIGURE 2-1. Assign statements.

```
                  / - - - - \
                 /           \
CAGE.1   -->   <     TIGER     >
                 \           /
                  \ - - - - /


                  / - - - - \
                 /           \
CAGE.2   -->   <     BEAR      >
                 \           /
                  \ - - - - /


                  / - - - - \
                 /           \
CAGE.3   -->   <     ZEBRA     >
                 \           /
                  \ - - - - /


                  / - - - - \
                 /           \
CRATE    -->   <  POLAR BEAR   >
                 \           /
                  \ - - - - /
```

In each case a variable name is given (e.g. CAGE.2) and is
assigned certain contents (e.g. the variable named CAGE.2 gets
<BEAR> as its contents).* The variable number of spaces around
the equals sign does not influence the assignments. All that is
important is that there be AT LEAST ONE space on either side of
this symbol. This equals sign is the most common of the SNOBOL
"operators". Such a symbol is called an operator because it
causes the assignment operation to take place.

It is also possible to build up a new variable from the contents of several other variables:

           ZOO = CAGE.1 CAGE.2 CAGE.3   (see Fig. 2-2)

                    FIGURE 2-2. Concatenation.

                    - - - - - - - - - - - - -
                  /   \
                /   \
ZOO   -->   <   TIGERBEARZEBRA   >
                \   /
                  \ - - - - - - - - - - - - - /

----
*In this chapter < and > will be used to enclose the exact con-
 tents of a variable so there will be no confusion about what a
 variable really contains.

This assign statement copies (but does not remove) the contents of
CAGE.1, CAGE.2, and CAGE.3 into ZOO. It´s like taking a picture
rather than an actual transfer. ZOO thus contains
<TIGERBEARZEBRA>.* Further it is possible to append things to a
variable which already has characters in it:

       ZOO = ZOO CRATE   (see Fig. 2-3)

FIGURE 2-3. Concatenation with old contents.

ZOO --> < TIGERBEARZEBRAPOLAR BEAR >

---

*Formally this combining of the contents of several variables into
one is called concatenation. Any variables or literals after the
equals sign are assigned as the contents of the variable before
the equals sign. These variables or literals (after the equals
sign) must be separated from one another by one or more blanks.

The equals sign here can be read as "set equal to" or "assign to".
It is not intended to indicate exact mathematical equality. After
the above statement has been executed, ZOO contains
<TIGERBEARZEBRAPOLAR BEAR>. If only ZOO = CRATE were used, the
contents of CRATE would replace the contents of ZOO. However,
when ZOO = ZOO CRATE, the old contents of ZOO are removed, held in
abeyance, combined with the contents of CRATE and reassigned to
ZOO.

  As this representation of animals is rather hard to read,
delimiting characters (separators) can be used by the programmer.
Spaces and commas are common delimiters. For example,

         ZOO = CAGE.1 ´,´ CAGE.2 ´,´ CAGE.3 ´,´ CRATE ´,´
                      (see Fig. 2-4)

         FIGURE 2-4. Concatenation using delimiters.

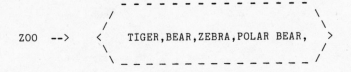

would give the variable ZOO the contents <TIGER,BEAR,ZEBRA,POLAR
BEAR,>. Here the literal commas in single quotes have been combined with the literal CONTENTS of CAGE.1, CAGE.2, CAGE.3 and
CRATE. In actuality the old contents of ZOO are completely erased
and these new contents put in. The fact that the contents are
similar in no way affects the erasure of all the old contents and
the insertion of new contents.

Table 2-1 has more examples of assign statements, and intro-
duces basic arithmetic in SNOBOL. In SNOBOL digits can be used
either as actual numbers or as symbols to be concatenated. See
the third through fifth lines of this table for an example of
these two qualitatively different forms of usage.

TABLE 2-1. Results of Assign Statements.

INITIAL CONTENTS OF BOX	STATEMENT(S)	RESULTING CONTENTS
anything	BOX = ´ABC´	<ABC>
<ABC>	BOX = ´PGN´	<PGN>
<PGN>	BOX = 9	<9>
<9>	BOX = BOX + 2	<11>
<11>	BOX = BOX ´ABC´	<11ABC>
<11ABC>	BOX = 5	<5>
<5>	BOX = ´4´	<4>
<4>	BOX = BOX + ´2´	<6>
<6>	BOX = BOX + 2	<8>

<8>	BOX = BOX ´2´	<82>
<82>	BOX = BOX 3	<823>
<823>	BOX = BOX + 7	<830>
<830>	BOX = "DOG"	<DOG>
<DOG>	BOX = BOX ´CAT´	<DOGCAT>
<DOGCAT>	BOX =	null
null	BOX = ´ ´	single space: < >
< >	BOX = "CAT" BOX ´DOG´	<CAT DOG>
<CAT DOG>	BOX = ´´	null*
null	C = ´,´ ; LET = ´A´ ; BOX = LET C LET C	<A,A,>
<A,A,>	LET = ´B´ ; BOX = LET ´-´ LET ´-´	<B-B->

MATCH STATEMENTS. The contents of a variable can be inspected with a match statement.

       ZOO ´GIBBON´

This statement asks if the literal characters <GIBBON> are contained IN THAT ORDER, WITH NO INTERVENING CHARACTERS, in the variable called ZOO. Matching proceeds in a left to right direction--but not necessarily at the beginning of the string of characters in a variable. The first occurrence of the characters sought after will satisfy the match.

    The above statement can either succeed or fail. The ZOO either has <GIBBON> or not. A SNOBOL program can be made to take note of this answer by using a "conditional goto".

---

*In this line of code, quotes do not enclose even a single space.

```
      ZOO 'GIBBON'       :S(NO.PURCHASE)
```

Here the program tells the computer to branch or go to a line with
a label of <NO.PURCHASE> if ZOO does in fact already contain
<GIBBON> thereby causing this statement to succeed. A branch to a
different part of the program based on the failure of this
matching statement could be stated as

```
      ZOO 'GIBBON'    :F(PURCHASE)
```

The "S" and "F" in these conditional gotos indicate success and
failure respectively. The statement

```
      ZOO 'EAR'    :S(LISTEN)
```

would be expected to fail with the contents of ZOO given earlier.
It would not, however, for ZOO really contains <EAR>--as the last
three characters of the first <BEAR>! This shows the need for
delimiters. The statement

```
      ZOO ',EAR,'    :S(LISTEN)
```

would fail because ZOO does not contain EXACTLY the sequence
<,EAR,>. Use of S and F gotos will be described more fully in the
next chapter.

   Match statements need not test just for literal characters.
They can also test if the contents of one variable are contained
in another variable.

```
      NEW.ANIMAL = 'GIBBON'
      ZOO NEW.ANIMAL    :F(PURCHASE)
```

is the same as

        ZOO ´GIBBON´ :F(PURCHASE)

The following examples show how gotos and match statements are
used in an actual program:

```
        ANIMAL.IN.CRATE  =  ´TIGER´
        ZOO ANIMAL.IN.CRATE      :S(END)
.PURCHASE  ZOO = ZOO  ´,´  ANIMAL.IN.CRATE
´END
```

As a result of this code, <,TIGER> would be added to ZOO if ZOO
did not already have a <TIGER> in it. Note that the second line
of this example makes this test, and as it is successful the
program branches to the END statement thereby skipping the PUR-
CHASE line.

Below, <,ZEBRA> would be added to ZOO if ZOO did not already
have a <ZEBRA> in it. As ZOO does have a <ZEBRA>, <NO> is
assigned as the value of DEALER.ANSWER, the program branches to
the END statement, and ZOO is unchanged.

```
        ANIMAL.ON.TRUCK = ´ZEBRA´
        ZOO ANIMAL.ON.TRUCK  :F(PURCHASE)
        DEALER.ANSWER = ´NO´   :(END)
PURCHASE ZOO = ZOO  ´,´  ANIMAL.ON.TRUCK
END
```

TABLE 2-2 shows the results of other match statements.

TABLE 2-2.   Results of Match Statements.

CONTENTS OF BOX		STATEMENT(S)	RESULTS S=success F=failure
anything		BOX ´´	S
<CAT>		BOX ´CAT´	S
<CATNIP>		BOX ´CAT´	S
<CATTLE>		BOX ´CAT´	S
<CART>		BOX ´CAT´	F
<CART>		BOX ´ART´	S
<CART>		BOX ´,ART,´	F
<APPLE>	LET = ´A´ ;	BOX LET	S
<APPLE>	LET = ´A´ ;	BOX LET ´P´	S
<APPLE>	LET = ´A´ ;	BOX LET ´L´	F
<APPLE>	LET = ´P´ ;	BOX ´A´ LET ´P´	S
<X+Y>		BOX ´+´	S
<X+Y>		BOX ´ ´	F
<X + Y>		BOX ´ ´	S
<X + Y>		BOX ´ ´	F

MATCH AND REPLACE STATEMENTS. In addition to just examining
the contents of a variable, it is possible to change these contents in the same statement. This is the purpose of the match and
replace statement.

        ZOO ´ZEBRA´ = ´RACCOON´

causes the contents of ZOO to become <TIGER,BEAR,RACCOON,POLAR
BEAR,>. The literal characters <ZEBRA> have been matched in ZOO
and replaced with the literal characters <RACCOON>. Characters
need not be replaced on a one-for-one basis; either more or less
characters can replace those matched. It is also important to
remember that EVERYTHING that is matched is replaced by what comes
after the equals sign. Thus

        ZOO ´ZEB´ ´RA´ = ´RACCOON´

would have accomplished the same thing as has just been done. The
combination of things which match in ZOO (i.e. <ZEB> and <RA>)
will be replaced by <RACCOON>.

    Match and replace statements can succeed or fail just as match
statements can; hence, they too can use gotos:

        ZOO ´PELICAN´ = ´PEACOCK´   :F(NO.BIRDS)

In this case the contents of ZOO remain unchanged as there is no
<PELICAN> in ZOO to replace. Thus the statement fails and the
program containing this statement branches to the line labeled
NO.BIRDS rather than the immediately following statement.

```
CAGE.4 = 'SEAL'
ZOO 'TIGER' = CAGE.4
```

The above two statements would delete <TIGER> from the variable
ZOO and replace it with <SEAL>, thus giving:
<SEAL,BEAR,RACCOON,POLAR BEAR,>. A match and replace statement
can therefore deal with both variables and literal characters.
Either one or both can be on either side of the equals sign.

An additional example of this usage would be:

```
OLD.CAGE = 'BEAR'
ZOO OLD.CAGE = 'LION'
```

These two statements would change ZOO to <SEAL,LION,RACCOON,POLAR
BEAR,>. If the match and replace statement were executed again
the <BEAR> in <POLAR BEAR> would be replaced and
<SEAL,LION,RACCOON,POLAR LION,> would result as the contents of
ZOO, since what the computer was seeking were the literal characters <BEAR>.

Hence it should not be forgotten that though SNOBOL can deal
with objects and concepts, it does not understand them. SNOBOL
treats the animals in the examples as just characters to be
manipulated.

A special form of the match and replace statement can be used
to remove something from a variable without putting anything in
its place.

```
ZOO 'POLAR LION' =
```

would correct the above error by removing <POLAR LION> from ZOO

and leave ZOO containing <SEAL,LION,RACCOON,,>. In effect <POLAR
LION> has been matched, and replaced with the "null string" (i.e.
nothing).

        ZOO WEIRD.ANIMAL =

would have accomplished the same thing if WEIRD.ANIMAL had previously been assigned <POLAR LION>.

The following code shows the combined use of all three kinds of
statements to check and possibly change the contents of a poker
hand.

```
        HAND = '3-C/4-H/5-D/6-S/6-D'
        NEXT.CARD = DRAW
        NEXT.CARD '2'   :S(KEEP.FOR.A.STRAIGHT)
        NEXT.CARD '7'   :F(END)
KEEP.FOR.A.STRAIGHT  HAND '6-D'  =  NEXT.CARD
END
```

In this example, the six of diamonds (6-D) is replaced by the
drawn card (DRAW) if this card is a 2 or a 7 of any suit. If not,
no change is made. In either case, the program ends up at the
statement labeled END. Note that if a 2 is found no test is made
for a 7 and the program jumps directly to KEEP.FOR.A.STRAIGHT.

Table 2-3 gives other illustrations of match and replace statements.

TABLE 2-3.   Results of Match and Replace Statements.

STARTING BOX CONTENTS	STATEMENT(S)	RESULTS & CONTENTS	
<RUBY>	BOX 'RUBY' = 'GLASS'	S	<GLASS>
<GLASS>	BOX 'GOLD' = 'LEAD'	F	<GLASS>
<GLASS>	BOX 'LASS' = 'LAD'	S	<GLAD>
<GLAD>	BOX 'GLAD' =	S	null
<79>	BOX '7' = '9'	S	<99>
<99>	BOX '99' = ' '	S	< >
< >	BOX ' ' =	S	null
<,123,124,125,>	BOX '12' = '13'	S	<,133,124,125,>
<,133,124,125,>	BOX '12' = '13'	S	<,133,134,125,>
<,133,134,125,>	BOX ',12,' = ',13,'	F	<,133,134,125,>
<,133,134,125,> as a group	/ C = ',' < BOX C = \ BOX C =	S S	<133134,125,>
<133134,125,>	BOX 31 = 99	S	<139934,125,>

A CAUTION.   Beginning programmers invariably make the mistake
of believing that because they select names which tell something
about the contents of a variable, the names in some way influence
those contents.   The fact that a box is called WEIRD.ANIMAL does
not mean that the computer knows there is no such thing as a polar
lion.   PRINT, NEXT, LIST, REPEAT, TALLY, WORD, LINE, COUNTER,
SAVE, COPY, LOOP, etc. are all legitimate names in SNOBOL.   Their
apparent meaning in no way affects execution, however.   DO NOT
FORGET THIS!   Unless told otherwise the programmer should assume

that all names he uses could be replaced by GOBBLEDYGOOK, for such a word has the same influence as LOOP or COUNTER.

There are two other parts to this caution. First the programmer should not go to the other extreme and use meaningless names. Though this may work, it would hardly make for a readable program. A programmer should choose meaningful, appropriate names fully realizing that these mnemonics don´t influence execution, but DO make it easier to comprehend a listing of the program.

The final part of this caution also causes beginners grief. There ARE some names in SNOBOL (often called reserved words) that DO have special functions as their names imply. Their inadvertent use often causes suprising and unwanted effects. INPUT, OUTPUT, END, REM, and RETURN are the most common of these.

EXERCISES

1. Write an assign statement which stores <FRENCH 101> in the variable COURSE.1.

2. Write an assign statement which puts <HISTORY 199> into COURSE.2.

3. Write a statement which concatenates the above two variables so that SCHEDULE contains <FRENCH 101, HISTORY 199>.

4. Write a statement which would direct a program to branch to NO.LANGUAGE if SCHEDULE did not contain <FRENCH>.

5. Write a statement which causes a program to go to
SOCIAL.SCIENCE.COURSES if SCHEDULE contains <HISTORY>.

6. If SCHEDULE still contains <FRENCH 101, HISTORY 199>, write a
statement which would replace <FRENCH 101> with <FRENCH 199>. Is
it necessary to use <FRENCH>? Why or why not?

7. If SCHEDULE now contains <FRENCH 199, HISTORY 199>, write a
statement which causes <HISTORY 199> to be replaced by <HISTORY
210>. In this case is it necessary to use <HISTORY>? Why or why
not?

8. Assume SCHEDULE now contains <FRENCH 199, HISTORY 210>, write
statements which ask if DROP contains <YES> and if it does delete
<HISTORY 210> from SCHEDULE; if not go to END.

Chapter 3.
SNOBOL Conventions and Techniques

Now with a feeling for the kinds of statements that exist, it is necessary to see precisely how SNOBOL statements are put together and assembled into a complete program. A number of rules or conventions exist which determine how a SNOBOL statement is entered on a punch card or typed in as a card image from a teletypewriter.

In addition to rules on statement construction it is necessary to know how to make a SNOBOL program communicate--in other words how it is possible to have the program read in data and print out results. Further, several techniques can be suggested for beginners which should decrease (but not eliminate) the number of errors they will make in learning and using SNOBOL.

>>> Putting Together a SNOBOL Statement

NAMING VARIABLES. Variable names can be up to 71 characters long. They can be composed of letters, numbers and/or periods in any order as long as a letter is the first character of the name. As has been mentioned, it is advisable to use names which are appropriate to the intended use of the variable. Periods are

commonly used to separate a variable name made up of several
words; the use of periods in no way affects the functioning of the
variable, however. WORD, NEXT.WORD, ITEM, ITEM.1, ITEM.2,
STRING.A, PATTERN.SIMPLE, PATTERN.DOUBLE, X, XX, LOOP.TALLY, V1,
V47, V765162482347343467967989......, Q........., F.......27, and
F.27. are all possible variable names. Though 71 characters may
be used, it usually becomes cumbersome if names are chosen which
have more than 10 or 12 characters--particularly if they are used
frequently in a program. Programmers should make a concerted
effort to choose relatively short names which will have meaning
not only to themselves but to others as well.

ALLOWABLE CHARACTERS. Any characters that can be punched or
typed can be used as literals or as the contents of SNOBOL
variables.* Letters, numbers, spaces, punctuation marks and
special symbols are all permissible. SNOBOL can also distinguish
between upper and lower case characters if the computer it runs on
has this capability. For example, all of the following are
acceptable:

        ABCabc12 34!@$%"´&=*+.

Some of these characters have special meanings within SNOBOL
(e.g. the equals sign causes assignment and the blank permits

----

*For all practical purposes a variable or a literal can contain as
many of these characters as desired. Several thousand are easily
accommodated as the contents of any given varaible or literal.
Because SNOBOL variables can hold these long strings of characters, they are often referred to as strings or string variables;
similarly literals are often called strings also.

concatenation), but nonetheless they can be assigned as the contents of a variable. When they are referred to literally in a
program they must be enclosed in quote marks. Both single and
double quotes can be used (if acceptable to the user's computer).
Consistency is required as illustrated below:

        CHARACTERS = ´23$%&´

  or

        CHARACTERS = "23$%&"

is acceptable, whereas

        CHARACTERS = ´23$%&"

  or

        CHARACTERS = "23$%&´

is not because the types of quotes around the literals do not
match. Single and double quotes are both legitimate literals if
they are set off by quotes of the opposite kind. For convenience
programmers sometimes make the following assignments:

        APOST =   "´"
        QUOTE =   ´"´

  STATEMENT LABELS. Labels are the names of places in a program.
A label is an optional name tag given to a statement so that other
statements can refer to the tagged or labeled statement.
  Labels can be composed of up to 72 letters, numbers and/or
periods. Either a letter or a number may start a label. Labels

must be started in column one of an 80 column card or in the first
position of a typed card image. START, BEGIN, NEXT.WORD, 100,
110, 9000000, P1, P3.5, LOOP.END, MORE, AGAIN, HERE, 2........,
and P......... are all legitimate labels.*

   GOTOS. Gotos are the last (optional) part of a statement.
They are indicators to jump or transfer to a part of the program
that has the label specified in the goto. They are placed last in
a statement. Gotos take one of four forms:

```
Unconditional goto:        :(label)

Go to on success:          :S(label)

Go to on failure:          :F(label)

Combined success or failure go to:
                           :S(label.1)F(label.2)
```

At least one space must come before the colon in the goto in order
to separate it from the rest of the statement. A goto cannot
extend beyond column 72.

   COMMENTS. Explanation or comments can be added to a SNOBOL
program. A comment line begins with an asterisk (*) in column
one. The remainder of the line is totally ignored by the computer
in executing the SNOBOL program. These starred lines are printed

---

*Beginning programmers are advised not to use labels which start
with a number as the technique of indirect reference is necessary
to branch to them (see Chapter 7).

with the listing of the program, however. A programmer should
adopt a consistent method of using comments. A typical technique
is to insert comments at the beginning of each logically different
section of the program. This not only gives an explanation of the
section but graphically sets it off from adjacent sections.

STATEMENT CONTINUATION. It is sometimes necessary to have a
statement which exceeds 72 columns. Such statements can be used
by being broken over several lines. This continuation is achieved
if a plus sign (+) is put in column one of each continuing line
after the line which starts the statement being continued. Statements can be broken wherever one or more blanks can be used (i.e.
not in the middle of a variable name). A literal can be broken
across lines, if the break point is closed with a quote mark and
restarted with a quote mark on the next line. For example:

```
*THIS CODE WHICH IS ASSUMED TO START IN COLUMN 1
*GIVES AN EXAMPLE OF SOME OF THE ABOVE POINTS.
     LOWER.CASE = ´abcdefghijklmnopqrstuvwxyz´
     LETTERS = LOWER.CASE "ABCDEFGHIJKLMNOP"
+    ´QRSTUVWXYZ´
```

The varaible called LETTERS now contains:

   <abcdefghijklmonpqrstuvwxyzABCDEFGHIJKLMNOPQRSTUVWXYZ>.

POSITIONING AND PACKING. With the exception of labels, which
if used must start in column one, SNOBOL code may be placed anywhere in the first 72 columns of a card or card image. Of course,
anything that starts in column one (unless it begins with a + or a
*) is assumed to be a label.

Lines of SNOBOL code need not contain a statement per se to
have a label or a goto. A line with just a label or just a goto
is perfectly acceptable. This kind of structuring is frequently
useful in a developing program where whole sections may be temporarily omitted and thus have their eventual presence indicated
by a label. Long lines can also have an unconditional goto placed
on the next line with no compromise in the logic of the program.
Frequently these techniques save repunching or retyping as a
program is being tested.

More than one statement can be placed in the first 72 columns
of a single line. This "packing" is accepted as long as adjacent
statements on the same line are separated by semicolons (;). The
first space after the semicolon is considered to be column one for
the next statement on that line; hence if a label is used for this
statement, it would follow the semicolon with no intervening
blanks:

statement.1   ;label   statement.2

>>> Input of Data; Output of Results

The reading in of data or the printing out of results is accomplished with specific kinds of assign statements.

Reading in: variable = INPUT

This causes a single 80 column card or card image to be read in
and become the contents of the variable to the left of the equals

sign. Each time "variable = INPUT" is used the next data card is
read in. A given data card can never be read more than once.
This special kind of input assignment fails when there is no more
data to process. Hence a typical statement in most SNOBOL programs is:

> variable = INPUT   :F(label)

where the label refers to a statement that handles the processing
that is to take place when all the data has been read in.

> Printing out: OUTPUT = variable

Here the contents of the variable to the right of the equals
sign are printed out on the computer's printer. As such printers
usually print 130 characters per line, the contents of a variable
are printed 130 characters at a time until all characters are
printed. Printing the contents of a variable does not change or
erase these contents.

If "PUNCH" is used instead of "OUTPUT" the contents of the
variable will be punched out on cards rather than printed. 80
characters per card are punched until all characters in the
variable have been processed. As with OUTPUT, "PUNCH = variable"
does not disturb the contents of the variable.

>>> Job Setup; Data Placement

Now that some of the SNOBOL conventions have been explained,
most prospective users are anxious to find out how to ACTUALLY RUN
a valid SNOBOL program on a real computer.   The following is a
fairly standard format for setting up a program.   Such a program
when submitted to a computer center is usually called a "job".
All of the system cards typically start in column one.

```
system job card

system card requesting SNOBOL execution


    .

    .    SNOBOL program (statements and comments)

    .


END (must start in column 1)


    .

    .    data if needed (can be read with INPUT)

    .


system end card
```

A user's computer center will show him the exact form the three
"system" cards depicted above should take.

>>> How To Keep SNOBOL from Snowballing

For the beginner to use SNOBOL efficiently, it is desirable to
give the computer certain overall instructions. These are
commonly included as the first three lines of the SNOBOL program.
They can start in any column AFTER column 1:

```
        &TRIM = 1
        &STLIMIT = 100
        &DUMP = 1
```

These three statements involve three SNOBOL keywords. Keywords
(which are discussed more fully in Chapter 8 and Appendix 1) are
variable names starting with an ampersand (&) which SNOBOL
reserves for special use.

&TRIM. Setting &TRIM to one causes all trailing blanks to be
trimmed from each card or card image which is read in as input.

```
            &TRIM = 1
            CARD = INPUT
        END
        ALBATROSS
```

In this case CARD contains only <ALBATROSS> and not <ALBATROSS>
followed by 71 spaces as it would have without the use of &TRIM.
Remember that data for a SNOBOL program can take up the full 80
columns of a card whereas the actual program statements are restricted to the first 72 columns of the card.

&STLIMIT.   STLIMIT is an abbreviation for statement limit.
Setting this keyword to 100 causes the termination of execution
after 100 statements have been executed.   This prevents a beginner
who has inadvertently programmed an unending repetition of statements (i.e. an unending loop) from executing many more statements
than he intends to--thereby ending his program only because he has
exceeded his time limit.   Besides just wasting time (and money)
such a termination usually deprives a programmer of any knowledge
of his program except that it ran too long.   Often a listing is
not even generated--let alone a dump (see below)--and he will have
great difficulty finding his error.

Of course when a program is expected to execute statements more
than 100 times, &STLIMIT can be set accordingly.   &STLIMIT does
not refer to the number of lines in a program but the total number
of times each statement is EXECUTED.   The idea that a statement
can be executed more than once (intentionally or not) is the idea
behind a loop (which will be discussed shortly).

&DUMP.   Setting &DUMP to one tells SNOBOL to print out or
"dump" the contents or structure of all nonnull variables at the
termination of the program.   Knowing the contents of all of these
variables is invaluable when errors have to be tracked down, an
activity called "debugging".

>>> An Example

To tie together the points made in this chapter, an actual
program and its results are presented. Figure 3-1 shows ALL the
cards which were used. Figure 3-2 shows what was printed by the
computer. This relatively simple program does nothing more than
replace "STOPS" with periods in a series of data cards to make the
assumed "telegram" more readable. The logic of this is quite
simple. Input is accomplished in Statement 4 (actually the eighth
line in Figure 3-2). Note that NEXT.LINE which starts in column
one of this line is the label for this statement. Statement 5
prints out what this input was. Note how the literal <ORIGINAL
LINE: > was concatenated with LINE to produce clearly identi-
fiable output. The heart of the program is Statement 6 which
branches back to itself until it has "matched and replaced" each
< STOP> with a <.>. This repetition is called a loop. Statements
7 and 8 (whose number is not indicated because it is packed with
7) print out the results and a blank line. Statement 9 loops back
to the beginning so that any remaining input can be processed.
When the input data is exhausted, the program jumps to the END in
Statement 10, produces a dump and terminates.

It should be stressed that the computer does NOT print out the
data which was read in unless the program is designed to do so.
It is for this reason that Figure 3-1 is provided so the actual
input can be examined. The unusual list generated in the dump
should not be disturbing; the presence of yet to be defined
variables and keywords occurs in all SNOBOL dumps.

FIGURE 3-1.   A SNOBOL program ready for running.

```
system job card
system card requesting SNOBOL execution
-LIST LEFT
**  ABOVE LINE PLACES STATEMENT NUMBERS ON THE LEFT.
    &DUMP = 1
    &STLIMIT = 100
    &TRIM = 1
**  THIS PROGRAM REPLACES THE "STOPS" IN A TELEGRAM
**  WITH PERIODS.
NEXT.LINE LINE = INPUT :F(END)
    OUTPUT = ´ORIGINAL LINE:  ´
+   LINE
MORE LINE ´ STOP´ = ´.´ :S(MORE)
    OUTPUT = ´NEW LINE:  ´ LINE ; OUTPUT = ´ ´
    :(NEXT.LINE)
END
ROSEMARY´S RED STOP TRICIA
IS BLUE STOP DICK´S BEEN
UNCOVERED STOP BUT THAT´S NOTHING NEW STOP
system end card
```

FIGURE 3-2.   Complete SNOBOL program output.

```
     -LIST LEFT
     **  ABOVE LINE PLACES STATEMENT NUMBERS ON THE LEFT.
1        &DUMP = 1
2        &STLIMIT = 100
3        &TRIM = 1
     **  THIS PROGRAM REPLACES "STOPS" IN A TELEGRAM
     **  WITH PERIODS.
4    NEXT.LINE LINE = INPUT :F(END)
5        OUTPUT = ´ORIGINAL LINE:  ´
5    +   LINE
6    MORE LINE ´ STOP´ = ´.´ :S(MORE)
7        OUTPUT = ´NEW LINE:  ´ LINE ; OUTPUT = ´ ´
9        :(NEXT.LINE)
10   END
ORIGINAL LINE:  ROSEMARY´S RED STOP TRICIA
NEW LINE:  ROSEMARY´S RED. TRICIA

ORIGINAL LINE:  IS BLUE STOP DICK´S BEEN
NEW LINE:  IS BLUE. DICK´S BEEN

ORIGINAL LINE:  UNCOVERED STOP BUT THAT´S NOTHING NEW STOP
NEW LINE:  UNCOVERED. BUT THAT´S NOTHING NEW.
```

DUMP OF VARIABLES AT TERMINATION

NATURAL VARIABLES

```
SUCCEED = PATTERN
INPUT = 'UNCOVERED STOP BUT THAT'S NOTHING NEW STOP'
LINE = 'UNCOVERED. BUT THAT'S NOTHING NEW.'
BAL = PATTERN
FAIL = PATTERN
OUTPUT = '  '
ABORT = PATTERN
FENCE = PATTERN
ARB = PATTERN
REM = PATTERN
```


UNPROTECTED KEYWORDS

```
&ABEND = 0
&ANCHOR = 0
&CODE = 0
&DUMP = 1
&ERRLIMIT = 0
&FTRACE = 0
&FULLSCAN = 0
&INPUT = 1
&MAXLNGTH = 5000
&OUTPUT = 1
&STLIMIT = 100
&TRACE = 0
&TRIM = 1
```


>>> Another Example

To further emphasize the basic aspects of programming in
SNOBOL, another complete program is presented in Figures 3-3 and
3-4. Figure 3-3 shows a listing of the input deck for the
computer's card reader; Figure 3-4 presents the output printed by
the computer's printer. This program reads in passenger names and
puts them in the nonsmoking section (i.e. assigns them to
NONSMOKING) unless (S) appears as part of the name--in which case,
they are put in the smoking section (i.e. assigned to SMOKING).

After all names have been read in, the two lists of passengers are
printed.

A powerful use of SNOBOL can be seen in statement 5 of this
program. Not only does this statement check for (S) to see if the
passenger smokes, but it also deletes these special characters at
the same time. Another feature of this code is the extensive use
of comment lines to separate the logical segments of the program.
Such a technique can be employed to advantage to make programs
clearer to their creators as well as to others who use them or
need to understand or modify them.

FIGURE 3-3.   Another SNOBOL program ready for running.

```
system job card
system card requesting SNOBOL execution
-LIST LEFT
*
*
******* INITIALIZE KEYWORDS *************************
*
    &DUMP = 1 ; &STLIMIT = 100 ; &TRIM = 1
*
*
******* READ IN PASSENGERS *************************
*
NEXT PASSENGER = INPUT :F(TAKE.OFF)
    PASSENGER '(S)' =    :S(SMOKES)
    NONSMOKING = NONSMOKING PASSENGER '  ' :(NEXT)
SMOKES SMOKING = SMOKING PASSENGER '  ' :(NEXT)
*
*
******* PRINT OUT PASSENGER LISTS ******************
*
TAKE.OFF OUTPUT = 'PASSENGERS IN SMOKING SECTION:'
         OUTPUT = SMOKING
         OUTPUT =
         OUTPUT = 'PASSENGERS IN NONSMOKING SECTION:'
         OUTPUT = NONSMOKING
END
HAAG(S)
WESSEL
DOBNICK
HUTCHINSON(S)
```

```
        OSTAPIK
        CHAMBERS
        WYNNE(S)
        system end card
```

FIGURE 3-4. Additional SNOBOL output.

```
      -LIST LEFT
      *
      *
      ******* INITIALIZE KEYWORDS *************************
      *
1         &DUMP = 1 ; &STLIMIT = 100 ; &TRIM = 1
      *
      *
      ******* READ IN PASSENGERS **************************
      *
4     NEXT PASSENGER = INPUT :F(TAKE.OFF)
5         PASSENGER '(S)' =    :S(SMOKES)
6         NONSMOKING = NONSMOKING PASSENGER ' ' :(NEXT)
7     SMOKES SMOKING = SMOKING PASSENGER ' '  :(NEXT)
      *
      *
      ******* PRINT OUT PASSENGER LISTS ******************
      *
8     TAKE.OFF OUTPUT = 'PASSENGERS IN SMOKING SECTION:'
9              OUTPUT = SMOKING
10             OUTPUT =
11             OUTPUT = 'PASSENGERS IN NONSMOKING SECTION:'
12             OUTPUT = NONSMOKING
13    END
```

```
PASSENGERS IN SMOKING SECTION:
HAAG  HUTCHINSON  WYNNE

PASSENGERS IN NONSMOKING SECTION:
WESSEL  DOBNICK  OSTAPIK  CHAMBERS


DUMP OF VARIABLES AT TERMINATION


NATURAL VARIABLES

SUCCEED = PATTERN
INPUT = 'WYNNE(S)'
BAL = PATTERN
FAIL = PATTERN
OUTPUT = 'WESSEL DOBNICK OSTAPIK CHAMBERS '
NONSMOKING = 'WESSEL DOBNICK OSTAPIK CHAMBERS '
```

```
ABORT = PATTERN
PASSENGER = ´WYNNE´
FENCE = PATTERN
ARB = PATTERN
REM = PATTERN
SMOKING = ´HAAG  HUTCHINSON  WYNNE

UNPROTECTED KEYWORDS

&ABEND = 0
&ANCHOR = 0
&CODE = 0
&DUMP = 1
&ERRLIMIT = 0
&FTRACE = 0
&FULLSCAN = 0
&INPUT = 1
&MAXLNGTH = 5000
&OUTPUT = 1
&STLIMIT = 100
&TRACE = 0
&TRIM = 1
```

EXERCISES

1. Identify any SNOBOL coding errors in the following statements.
The S in START in statement a. defines column 1.

a.   START TEXT = OUTPUT

b.   INPUT =TEXT

c.   INPUT =TEXT   OLD.TEXT   :F(END)

d.   TEXT =   INPUT   ;F(END)

e.   TEXT=INPUT   ;   :F(END)

f.   TEXT = INPUT :S(END)

g.   TEXT =   ;OUTPUT = INPUT

h.   TEXT = ;   OUTPUT=INPUT

i.   TEXT/OLD   =   INPUT

j.   TEXT = OLD/   INPUT

```
k.            TXET = 'FISH'

l.   TEXT = TEXT INPUT  :F(MORE.PROCESSING)

m.     X = 47 ; B = 95.2 ; WORD = 23.895 ; REAL.WORD = 0.56

n.     WORD = 'NUMBERS' AND DIGITS'

o.     WORD = 'DOG' ;WORD = "CAT" ; WORD = ;THE.BEGINNING

p.   NOW TEXT = TEXT INPUT :F(MORE)S(NOW)

q.   NO.MORE.TEXT TEXT = TEXT INPUT :S(NO.MORE.TEXT)

r.            &DUMP = 0

s.            &STLIMIT = 250

t.            &TRIM = TEXT INPUT :F(END.IT)

u.            &TRIM.SOME.MORE.TEXT = INPUT  :F(MORE.TRIMMINGS)

v.   CORRECT.VARIABLE = 'THIS IS OK'

w.            CARDS = '3-C/4-H/27-D'

x.            AMAZON.JUNGLE = 'POLAR BEAR'

y.   BAD.CHARACTERS = '    $'%'&(')('('(')"'

z.   +        'THIS IS THE REST OF THE TEXT.'

aa.           PUNCH = INPUT 'CARD.CODE'

bb.           OUTPUT = "SYSTEM end card"

cc.  END

dd.           TEXT "THE END IS NEAR"  = 'END' :F(THE.ABSOLUTE.END
```

2. Write a SNOBOL program which prints out the message, THIS IS A
SIMPLE SNOBOL PROGRAM.

3. Write a SNOBOL program which prints a line of data read in
from a card image. The card image contains, THIS CAME FROM A DATA
IMAGE.

4A.   Write a SNOBOL program which assigns LEAD to a variable, asks
if the variable contains GOLD and branches to print, I DIDN´T FIND
IT.

4B.   Write a SNOBOL program which assigns GOLD to a variable, asks
if the variable contains GOLD and branches to print, EUREKA, I
FOUND IT.

4C.   Write a program combining 4A and 4B which reads in LEAD, MUD,
IRON, GOLD, LIMESTONE, and PYRITES (each from a separate card
image) and prints I DIDN´T FIND IT or EUREKA, I FOUND IT. based on
whether the input is GOLD or not.

5.   Write a SNOBOL program which prints a variable´s contents,
replaces one thing in the variable with something else and then
prints the resulting contents. Use your imagination to create
interesting contents.

6.   Write a program which reads in four objects from separate
cards; stores them all in a variable and then deletes from the
variable the object that appears on the fifth data card. Use the
following five objects: PEACH, APRICOT, PEA, CUCUMBER, PEA. Be
sure the program prints out the initial contents and the final
contents of the variable.

7.   Write a program which changes the part numbers on inventory
control cards. The revised cards should be punched as well as

printed. Specifically, the program should change part numbers
with JX to JA and change PQ to P-27. For example, JX9348 WING
NUTS/100 would become JA9348 WING NUTS/100; 938PQ TUBING(10´)
would become 938P-27 TUBING(10´), etc. Use at least five different cards.

8. Take the cards generated above and write a program which moves
all the information over 10 columns and punches the date in the
first 8 columns of the card. Month, day, and year should each
come in on separate cards (as the first data read). The program
should insert slashes so that the result looks like:

        01/15/75   JA9348 WING NUTS/100

9. Write a program which reads in the following objects and puts
them into DRAWER. The first time a duplicate object is found, add
an "S" to the old object already in DRAWER. Additional duplicates
cause no change. The final contents of DRAWER are to be printed
out at the end of the program.

        PEN   PEN
        ERASER   ERASER
        PENCIL   PAPER CLIP
        INK   PAPER
        PEN   PEN
        PENCIL   PAPER CLIP

Be sure to read in the first column before the second.

Chapter 4.
Pattern Matching in SNOBOL

Up to now, match and match and replace statements have been used to look for patterns composed only of sequential strings of characters. However, many patterns already exist in SNOBOL which make matching much more powerful and flexible. To understand this power and flexibility, it is necessary to think of patterns which "don´t know precisely what they are looking for"--as do the literals and variables in match and match and replace statements which have been considered so far. For example, imagine a line of 100 people as similar to a SNOBOL string variable. All matching of literals and variables can do is operate on specific people in this line:

    Is Harry Parker there?
    Replace Cindy with Alice.
    Can Helen be found?
    Substitute Capt. Connors for Sgt. Riley.

The patterns which will be described in this chapter allow asking much more:

    Find the first woman in the line.
    Take the first ten people.

52

Replace the last fifty people with 25
school children.

Take everyone after the first woman with
blue eyes but before the first man with red hair.

Take people only until the first person less than
5´ tall is found.

Find the first man who weighs more than 200
pounds or who is more than 6´5" tall.

Analogous questions can be asked about characters and groups of
characters in a SNOBOL string variable. BREAK(), SPAN(), LEN(),
ARB, REM and alternation are the patterns which do this. They and
their uses are the subject of this chapter.

There are essentially two kinds of patterns in SNOBOL:
functions and so called "built-in" patterns. Both of these can
match various things in a SNOBOL string variable; functions,
however, allow an "argument" or specification of conditions or
particular things which should or shouldn´t be matched. Though
more details about functions can be found in a later chapter, it
is sufficient here to realize that patterns lack parentheses while
functions do not, as shown below:

```
function(argument(s))
```

For all practical purposes the functions and patterns to be
described here behave in essentially the same way; they are
special words or abbreviations which can be used in both match and
match and replace statements to match almost any pattern a
programmer can define. The following subset of SNOBOL patterns
and functions suffices for most basic and many sophisticated

SNOBOL programs. (A list of all other patterns and functions is
provided in Appendix 2)

>>> A Basic Subset of Patterns and Functions

BREAK(). In scanning from left to right, BREAK(character(s))
matches characters in a string up to but not including whichever
of the characters in its argument is encountered first. Some
examples of its use:

     STRING BREAK(´,´)

Here everything up to but not including the first comma in the
variable STRING is matched.

     STRING BREAK(´ ´)

In this case, everything up to the first blank is matched.

     SENTENCE BREAK(´,.?:;!´)

In the variable SENTENCE everything up to but not including the
first of various punctuation marks is matched. A comma need not
be the first punctuation mark in SENTENCE. This match statement
will succeed if a period, question mark, or other given punctuation is encountered first.

     DELIMITER = ´-/´ ; STRING BREAK(DELIMITER)

With the variable DELIMITER as the argument for BREAK(), everything up to but not including a slash or a dash is matched. It
doesn´t matter which one is encountered first in STRING; whatever

occurs from the beginning of STRING to this character is matched
by BREAK(DELIMITER).

ALPHABET 'D' BREAK('Q')

In the above example, matching does not necessarily start at
the beginning of the variable ALPHABET. Here whatever occurs
after the first D is matched up to but not including a Q. If the
variable ALPHABET does contain the usual 26 letters, BREAK('Q')
would match EFGHIJKLMNOP. It is important to remember that
BREAK() does not match any of the characters in its argument (i.e.
in the literal or variable that is enclosed in parentheses after
BREAK). Of course, if none of BREAK()'s arguments are in the
string, the whole match fails.

```
PHRASE = 'THE FAT CAT'
PHRASE BREAK(' ') = 'A'
```

Patterns and functions can be used in match and replace statements. Here THE FAT CAT becomes A FAT CAT. BREAK(' ') matched
THE and it was replaced with A. Table 4-1 gives further examples
of BREAK().

TABLE 4-1. Uses of BREAK().

In each example, BREAK() by itself matches the underlined
characters. (Note that the object being scanned is a literal.)

´RED, YELLOW, & GREEN´   BREAK(´,´)

´RED, YELLOW, & GREEN´   BREAK(´ ´)

´RED, YELLOW, & GREEN´   BREAK(´&´)

´RED, YELLOW, & GREEN´   BREAK(´,&´)

´RED, YELLOW, & GREEN´   BREAK(´&,´)

´RED, YELLOW, & GREEN´   ´&´ BREAK(´N´)

SPAN(). SPAN(character(s)) matches all continuing characters
in a variable as long as they are identical to one of the characters in its argument. Specific examples are shown below:

LINE SPAN(´ ´)

Here the first run of blanks is matched. The match continues
until a nonblank character is found. A blank need not be the
first character in LINE.

WORD SPAN(´AEIOU´)

In this case an uninterrupted string of vowels is matched
(starting with the first vowel encountered). As with BREAK(), the
A which is the first character of SPAN()´s argument need not be
the first vowel encountered. Again like BREAK(), SPAN() works
from left to right.

        WORD BREAK(´ ´) SPAN(´ ´) BREAK(´ ´)

In the above example, the two BREAK(´ ´)s match groups of
charcters separated by a variable number of blanks (which are
matched by SPAN(´ ´)). More specifically:

        WORD = ´MEASLES´
        VOW = ´AEIOU´
        WORD BREAK(VOW) SPAN(VOW) BREAK(VOW)

The first BREAK(VOW) matches M (i.e. everything up to a vowel).
SPAN(VOW) matches EA (i.e., all uninterrupted vowels). Thirdly,
the last BREAK(VOW) matches SL which is everything up to E which
is the next vowel. Thus the resulting matched values are,
consecutively, M, EA, AND SL. This example shows that one
function cannot match what has already been matched by another
function or pattern. Matching must always be consecutive, and two
patterns cannot match the same thing.

        TEXT = ´   MAN, AM I SPACED OUT´
        TEXT SPAN(´ ´) =

Here the eight initial blanks in TEXT are matched and deleted
(i.e. matched and replaced with nothing). One, two, one hundred
or more uninterrupted blanks could be deleted by this statement.
Table 4-2 gives more examples of SPAN().

TABLE 4-2. Uses of SPAN().

In each example, SPAN() by itself matches the underlined
characters. (Note that the object being scanned is a literal.)

´RED, XXXXXX, & GREEN´   SPAN(´X´)

´RED, XXXXXX, & GREEN´   SPAN(´X ,´)

´RED, XXXXXX, & GREEN´   SPAN(´& ,X´)

´RED, XXXXXX, & GREEN´   SPAN(´E´)
  -

´RED, XXXXXX, & GREEN´   SPAN(´DER´)

´RED, XXXXXX, & GREEN´   ´E´ SPAN(´E´)
                       -

LEN(). LEN(n) matches something that is n characters long.
LEN stands for length. Some of its uses are:

          NUMBER LEN(5)

LEN(5) matches the first five characters in NUMBER. If NUMBER
were numeric, LEN(5) would match the first five digits in NUMBER.
A decimal point might also be matched if it were among the first
five characters.

          N = 10 ; STRING LEN(N)

The first 10 characters in STRING are matched.

BOX ´,´ LEN(4)

Here the first four characters AFTER the first comma are
matched. Though a comma need not be the first character in BOX,
the match must start with a comma. Any match using LEN() fails if
it cannot find the required number of characters.

BOX LEN(4) ´,´

Now four characters BEFORE the first comma are matched. If
there aren´t four characters before the first comma, a comma is
sought which does have four characters before it. If no such
comma is found, the match statement fails.

STRING LEN(NUMBER)

The value assigned to NUMBER determines how many characters are
matched starting with the first one in STRING. As with all uses
of LEN(), its argument must be a whole integer number. Zero is
acceptable, but negative or decimal values are not.

```
RUN.CARD = ´/LOGON MY JOB´
RUN.CARD ´/´ LEN(5) = ´/LOGOFF´
```

The LOGON in RUN.CARD has been replaced with LOGOFF. Note that
matching the slash required that the slash also be used on the
right of the equals sign so the desired result of /LOGOFF MY JOB
could be achieved. Table 4-3 shows additional examples of LEN().

TABLE 4-3. Uses of LEN().

In each example, LEN() by itself matches the underlined
characters. (Note that the object being scanned is a literal.)

´RED, YELLOW, & GREEN´   LEN(10)

N = 10
´RED, YELLOW, & GREEN´   LEN(N)

´RED, YELLOW, & GREEN´   LEN(´10´)

´RED, YELLOW, & GREEN´   ´,´ LEN(4)

´RED, YELLOW, & GREEN´   ´W,´ LEN(4)

´RED, YELLOW, & GREEN´   LEN(4) ´,´

´RED, YELLOW, & GREEN´   LEN(2) ´,´
  --

´RED, YELLOW, & GREEN´   BREAK(´ ´) ´ ´ LEN(6)

´RED, YELLOW, & GREEN´   ´&´ LEN(10)
      match fails

´RED, YELLOW, & GREEN´   LEN(20) ´&´
      match fails

ARB. ARB matches nothing or as much of anything necessary to make other patterns or characteristics match. ARB stands for arbitrary. Some examples of ARB:

LIST ´,´ ARB ´,´

Here ARB matches anything between the first two commas in LIST. If there is nothing between these commas, ARB matches the null string. If LIST contains less than two commas, this match would fail.

BOX ´,´ ARB

In this statement, ARB matches the null string because this is all that is needed to insure that the rest of the pattern (i.e. the single comma) matches.

CODE ´/´ ARB ´+´ = ´/SQRT(X)+´

All characters in CODE between the first slash and a following plus sign are matched and replaced with SQRT(X). Of course this slash and the plus are also matched, but since they are replaced by a slash and a plus respectively, it appears as if only the characters between them are matched and replaced.* Table 4-4 illustrates the workings of ARB.

---

*Though ARB is quite powerful, it is also somewhat inefficient; hence, as your SNOBOL programming knowledge advances you will find alternatives to ARB.

TABLE 4-4. Uses of ARB.

In each example, ARB by itself matches the underlined
characters. (Note that the object being scanned is a literal.)

´RED, YELLOW, & GREEN´   ´,´ ARB ´,´

´RED, YELLOW, & GREEN´   ´,´ ARB ´&´

´RED, YELLOW, & GREEN´   ´&´ ARB
 ARB matches nothing

´RED, YELLOW, & GREEN´   ARB ´&´
 ARB matches nothing

´RED, YELLOW, & GREEN´   BREAK(´,´) ARB ´&´

´RED, XXXXXX, & GREEN´   SPAN(´X´) ARB ´N´

´RED, XXXXXX, & GREEN´   SPAN(´X´) ARB ´EN´

´RED, XXXXXX, & GREEN´   SPAN(´X´) ARB ´NE´
      match fails

REM. REM matches the remainder of what can be matched in a
variable. After other patterns in a statement have matched
something, REM matches what remains proceeding in a left to right
direction. It doesn´t back up over what has already been matched.
Uses of REM:

SENTENCE ´,´ REM

Here REM matches everything after the first comma in SENTENCE.

     STRING.VARIABLE LEN(4) REM

In this example, REM matches everything in STRING.VARIABLE
except the first four characters.

     SENTENCE ´;´ REM = ´;´ NEW.PHRASE

In this match and replace statement the contents of NEW.PHRASE
replace whatever came after the first semicolon in SENTENCE.
Table 4-5 shows some typical uses of REM.

TABLE 4-5.   Uses of REM.

In each example, REM by itself matches the underlined
characters. (Note that the object being scanned is a literal.)

   ´RED, YELLOW, & GREEN´   ´,´ REM

   ´RED, YELLOW, & GREEN´   LEN(6) REM

   ´RED, YELLOW, & GREEN´   ´&´ REM

   ´RED, YELLOW, & GREEN´   REM ´&´
      match fails

ALTERNATION. It is now possible to look for a variety of patterns in a variable. Strings can be searched up to or through given characters using BREAK() and SPAN(); strings composed of something, anything and something can be matched with patterns containing ARB; specific parts of a string can be matched with LEN() and REM; and, of course, something and something and something else can be matched with simple concatenation of literals and/or variables.

The fundamental operation which is not possible yet is alternation or ORing. Does a variable contain something OR something OR something else. To search for alternate possibilities requires a new SNOBOL operator: the vertical bar or alternation symbol (|). It must always be delimited by at least one space on either side. Some examples using this symbol are shown below:

        ZOO ´LION´ | ´TIGER´

Here either LION or TIGER--whichever occurs first in ZOO--is matched.

        MORE PARAGRAPH ´, AND ´ | ´, BUT ´ = ´; ´ :S(MORE)

In this example which loops back upon itself via the label MORE, all the clauses in PARAGRAPH which are joined by a comma and AND or BUT have this connection replaced with a semicolon. This one statement repeatedly executes itself until it has found all such occurrences. The ANDs and BUTs can be in any order and any frequency, but this one statement will replace them all.

EQUATION EXPRESSION.1 | EXPRESSION.2 = ´X´

Here an X replaces EXPRESSION.1 or EXPRESSION.2--whichever is found first going from left to right--in EQUATION. More examples of alternation can be found in Table 4-6.

TABLE 4-6. Patterns Matched By Alternation (|).

In each example, the pattern enclosed in parentheses matches the underlined characters. (Note that the object being scanned is a literal.)

´RED, YELLOW, & GREEN´   (´RED´ | ´GREEN´)

´RED, YELLOW, & GREEN´   (´GREEN´ | ´RED´)

´RED, YELLOW, & GREEN´   (´GREEN´ | ´YELLOW´)

´RED, YELLOW, & GREEN´   (´GREEN´ | ´YELLOW´ | ´RED´)

´27 REDS & 144 GREENS´   (´271´ | ´714´)
  match fails

´27 REDS & 144 GREENS´   (´144´ | ´27´)
 --

´27 REDS & 144 GREENS´   (27 | 144)
 --

´27 REDS & 144 GREENS´   (4 | 7)
  -

´27 REDS & 144 GREENS´   (72 | 144)

>>> User-Defined Patterns

    Frequently a given pattern is used many times in a program, and
as it is bothersome and potentially error-producing to type
quotes, parentheses, etc. repeatedly, SNOBOL allows a pattern to
be assigned as the contents of a variable:

        ┌─────────────────────────┐
        │   variable = pattern   │
        └─────────────────────────┘

Once a programmer defines a variable as a pattern, he can use it
as being equivalent to this pattern until he assigns something new
to the variable.   Examples of user-defined patterns:

        EVEN.DIGITS = 0 | 2 | 4 | 6 | 8
    EVEN.DIGITS is now a pattern which matches any even digit.

        VOWELS = ´A´ | ´E´ | ´I´ | ´O´ | ´U´
    VOWELS will now match the first vowel it finds in a string; it
need not be an A.

        INCLUSIVE = ´(´ ARB ´)´
    INCLUSIVE is now defined to be a pattern which will match
anything enclosed in parentheses including the parentheses themselves.   Note that ARB itself does not match the parentheses.

        RAPTOR = ´OWL´ | ´HAWK´ | ´EAGLE´ | ´VULTURE´
        BIRD.CHECK.LIST RAPTOR :S(BIRD.OF.PREY)
    Here a pattern is set up which scans BIRD.CHECK.LIST for any
one of the four birds of prey.   If one is found, the program goes

to the statement labeled BIRD.OF.PREY. When a variable such as
RAPTOR which contains a pattern is listed in a SNOBOL dump, its
contents are indicated as PATTERN--not the actual pattern itself
(cf. Figures 3-2 and 3-4).

>>> Conditional Value Assignment

Checking for patterns is a powerful part of SNOBOL, but hopefully it has left the programmer feeling something is missing.
Checking for complex, alternating patterns, ten characters into a
string after a blank is fine, but who knows what was matched. S
and F gotos can isolate two possibilities, but this is quite
inadequate for a variable whose contents are essentially unknown
(e.g. text which has come in as input data). This problem is
solved with the method of conditional value assignment.

A variable can be assigned what a pattern matches. The new
operator needed for this technique is the period (.). As with
the alternation operator, the period must be surrounded by at
least one blank on each side. The general format for conditional
value assignment:

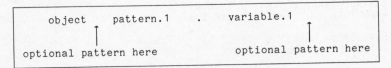

The period between pattern.1 and variable.1 is the conditional
value assigment operator. It causes whatever pattern.1 matches in
object--and ONLY what pattern.1 matches--to become the contents of

variable.1.   If the match fails, the contents of variable.1 remain
unchanged from what they were before this statement was executed.
This is what is meant by the term conditional: the value assignment is conditional on the success of the whole match--including
the successful matching of any other patterns which may be present.   Table 4-7 shows the results of a number of different statements using conditional value assignment.

    TABLE 4-7.   Examples of Conditional Value Assignment.

    In each example below, STRING is assumed to contain
"CONDITIONAL VALUE ASSIGNMENT WORKS; USE IT!".   The result of each
conditional value assignment is indicated after each statement.

```
    STRING BREAK(´;´) . RESULT
    RESULT is assigned:  ´CONDITIONAL VALUE ASSIGNMENT WORKS´

    STRING BREAK(´ ´) . RESULT
    RESULT is assigned:  ´CONDITIONAL´

    STRING (BREAK(´ ´) ´ ´) . RESULT
    RESULT is assigned:  ´CONDITIONAL ´

    STRING BREAK(´/´) . RESULT
    RESULT is unchanged because the match fails

    STRING BREAK(´;´) REM . RESULT
    RESULT is assigned:  ´; USE IT!´

    STRING ´;´ LEN(3) . RESULT ARB ´!´
    RESULT is assigned:  ´ US´

    STRING BREAK(´;´) . RESULT REM =
    RESULT is assigned:  ´CONDITIONAL VALUE ASSIGNMENT WORKS´
    STRING is set to null
```

```
(STRING '/') BREAK('/') . RESULT
```
RESULT is assigned everything in STRING. Note how STRING
was concatenated with a literal slash to form the subject
of this match statement.

```
STRING 'C' | 'T' . RESULT
```
RESULT is assigned: 'T'

```
STRING ('C' | 'T') . RESULT
```
RESULT is assigned: 'C'

```
STRING BREAK(';') . RESULT '!'
```
RESULT is unchanged because the match fails

```
STRING '; ' REM . RESULT = RESULT
```
RESULT is assigned: 'USE IT!'
STRING now contains: 'USE IT!'

```
STRING LEN(4) . RESULT.1 LEN(3) . RESULT.2
```
RESULT.1 is assigned: 'COND'
RESULT.2 is assigned: 'ITI'

```
STRING BREAK(';') . R.1 '; ' ARB . R.2 '!' = R.2 '; ' R.1 '.'
```
R.1 is assigned: 'CONDITIONAL VALUE ASSIGNMENT WORKS'
R.2 is assigned: 'USE IT'
STRING now contains: 'USE IT; CONDITIONAL VALUE
ASSIGNMENT WORKS.'

The following complete program with conditional value assignment uses the BREAK() function to define the pattern to be
matched. In this program textual data is read in a line at a time
and stored in TEXT. When the input is exhausted, a branch is
taken to PROCESS and LIST is set up containing all the unique
words in TEXT.

```
            &TRIM = 1
            LIST = '/'
    *
    *
    ******* READ IN TEXT *********************************
    *
    MORE LINE = INPUT :F(PROCESS)
         TEXT = TEXT LINE ' ' :(MORE)
    *
    *
    ******* DELETE MULTIPLE BLANKS & COMMON PUNCTUATION **
    *
    PROCESS TEXT ' ' = ' ' :S(PROCESS)
    MARKS TEXT '.' | ',' | ';' | ':' | '?' = :S(MARKS)
    *
    *
    ******* MAKE LIST OF UNIQUE WORDS ********************
    *
    NEXT.WORD TEXT BREAK(' ') . WORD ' ' = :F(READY.PRINT)
         LIST '/' WORD '/' :S(NEXT.WORD)
         LIST = LIST WORD '/' :(NEXT.WORD)
    ** THE SLASH USED IN THE ABOVE TWO STATEMENTS
    ** SERVES AS A DELIMITER FOR THE WORDS IN LIST.
    *
    *
    ******* PRINT UNIQUE WORDS **************************
    *
    READY.PRINT LIST '/' =
    PRINT.LIST LIST BREAK('/') . OUTPUT '/' =
    +   :S(PRINT.LIST)
    END

    THIS PROGRAM WILL PICK OUT ALL THE UNIQUE WORDS
    IN THESE THREE LINES OF INPUT DATA AND PRINT
    THEM IN ONE VERTICAL LIST.
```

Conditional value assignment is used twice in this program. In
the line labeled NEXT.WORD, the period operator assigns to WORD
whatever BREAK(' ') matches. Unless TEXT contains some unusual
characters or punctuation, WORD should contain one word, for the
lines of code from PROCESS to NEXT.WORD have removed punctuation
and multiple spacing. Special attention should be given to the
use of the blank as the delimiting character in this line. As
BREAK(' ') does not match the blank it must be matched by ' ', and

this in addition to what BREAK(´ ´) matches are both deleted from TEXT. The fact that WORD is assigned a value does not influence the deletion because the assignment takes place before the deletion.

This use of delimiters is also important in the PRINT.LIST line where BREAK() and the period operator are used to remove words from LIST and cause them to be printed (one per line) by assigning them to OUTPUT. The slashes which are used as delimiters in LIST are not printed because they are deleted from LIST and not matched by BREAK(). The slashes are here, of course, so the words in LIST can be separated from one another and broken off LIST one at a time. The slashes also serve to insure that only exact words will be matched (by LIST ´/´ WORD ´/´ :S(NEXT.WORD)). If slashes were not used to delimit all of the words, this statement would succeed if it found THE as part of THERE. This is also the reason the second line of code assigns a single slash to LIST: even the first word needs to be surrounded by slashes. Note that this first slash is later deleted in READY.PRINT so BREAK(´/´) will not match the null string before this initial character.*

SPAN(), as well as BREAK(), can be used very effectively with conditional value assignment. In the following four-statement example, votes are extracted from a list of candidates who received them. The votes are then summed to determine the turnout for the election.

---

*An alternate way of writing a program which handles many lines of textual data is to process each line as it comes in as input. No long string like TEXT need ever be used. This method can save computer time in most SNOBOL implementations where a string such as TEXT is stored anew each time it is changed.

```
NEXT INPUT SPAN(1234567890) . VOTES  :F(PRINT.TOTAL)
      TOTAL = TOTAL + VOTES  :(NEXT)
PRINT.TOTAL OUTPUT   =   'TOTAL='  TOTAL
END
TRAVIS     123
ORCHARD=103
410 FOR OLSON
988-JACOBSON
17/FIRESTONE
CRARY HAS 505
```

When run, this program prints TOTAL=2146.

Several things have been done in this example which merit special consideration. First, SPAN() with the ten digits as its argument has been used to match the first continuous string of digits found on an input card (i.e. the number of votes the candidate got). This number can be of any length and appear anywhere on the card--before or after the candidate's name with any intervening characters other than a digit. Also of importance in this example is the use of INPUT as the subject of a pattern match. Each time this statement is executed, a new card is read and assigned as the value of INPUT.

Often a pattern match and conditional value assignment can be accomplished in several different ways. Consider the task of straightening out a person's full name which has been entered with the last name first (e.g. JONES, JOHN PAUL). Assuming there may be initial blanks, this name could be put in order with the following code:

```
  &TRIM = 1
  NAME = INPUT
  NAME SPAN(' ') BREAK(',') . LAST ', '
+ REM . FIRST.AND.MIDDLE
  NAME = FIRST.AND.MIDDLE ' ' LAST
```

SPAN(´ ´) matches the initial blanks (if any), BREAK(´,´) matches
the last name, and REM picks up the first and middle names.
Conditional value assignment saves the names which have been
matched, and concatenation then achieves the desired order.

More simply this could be done with just one conditional value
assignment:

```
&TRIM = 1
NAME = INPUT
NAME SPAN(´ ´) BREAK(´,´) . LAST ´, ´ =
NAME = NAME ´ ´ LAST
```

Here the initial blanks and the last name are deleted from NAME
leaving the first and middle names which then can be concatenated
with LAST.

This code could be further condensed by combining the matching,
assignment, and replacement into one statement:

```
  &TRIM = 1
  NAME = INPUT
  NAME SPAN(´ ´) BREAK(´,´) . LAST ´, ´
+ REM . FIRST.AND.MIDDLE = FIRST.AND.MIDDLE ´ ´ LAST
```

It is important to realize here that LAST and FIRST.AND.MIDDLE are
given values BEFORE replacement happens.

Lastly, one more statement could be dropped. Replacing NAME
with INPUT leaves only two statements. In this case, INPUT functions as it did in the vote tallying example:

```
  &TRIM = 1
  INPUT SPAN(´ ´) BREAK(´,´) . LAST ´, ´
+ REM . FIRST.AND.MIDDLE = FIRST.AND.MIDDLE ´ ´ LAST
```

A caution is in order here. Despite the fact that this last
example is quite compact, it is not necessarily desirable. Though

it will result in some savings in terms of computer time, it will
probably be harder to understand than any of the other examples.
This issue of compactness must be carefully considered by SNOBOL
programmers. Efficiency gained by using powerful compact statements must always be weighed against their clarity.

Sometimes--though not always--a programmer himself can get con-
fused by a complex statement he has just written, and would have
been better off with several simpler statements.

   PREDEFINED CONDITIONAL VALUE ASSIGNMENT. Conditional value
assignment can also be PREDEFINED.* This means that a special
pattern can be set up in advance so that whatever it matches is
assigned to a variable. In the example on page 70, the following
line of code could be placed at the beginning of the program:

        BEFORE.BLANK.INTO.WORD = (BREAK(´ ´) . WORD) ´ ´

BEFORE.BLANK.INTO.WORD is now a user-defined pattern which matches
something up to a blank and then the blank. Further, whatever it
matched before the blank is assigned as the contents of WORD. The
parentheses surrounding BREAK(´ ´) . WORD are not really needed,
but they help clarify what is happening. With
BEFORE.BLANK.INTO.WORD now defined in this way the NEXT.WORD line
in the program could be changed to:

_____

*The remainder of this chapter can be skipped at the first
 reading.

```
        NEXT.WORD BEFORE.BLANK.INTO.WORD = :F(READY.PRINT)
```

This has not changed what the program does, but it has simplified
this line of code. Such simplification is really desirable only
if the user-defined pattern used in predefined conditional value
assignment is used more than once, for using it only once isn't
very efficient since an extra line has been added to the program
with no resulting simplification.

>>> The Cursor Position Operator (@)

   A very handy thing to know about a match is precisely where in
a string it took place. This is the function of @ (the "at"
sign). By prefacing a variable with @ in a pattern match, the
variable is set so it matches nothing (i.e. it in no way affects
the rest of the match). What happens to this variable is very
useful, however. This variable is assigned the numerical character position of the imaginary scanner or cursor that has been
moved over the string being examined. The value for the
@variable, the so-called "at-variable," is the character position
that was scanned when the @variable was encountered. Some
examples should make this clear:

```
        ANIMAL = 'CAT'
        ANIMAL 'A' @PLACE
        OUTPUT = PLACE
```

The integer 2 will be printed out by this code as the match
stopped in the second position in the variable being matched. If
the second line of this code were changed to:

```
      ANIMAL @PLACE 'A'
```

1 would be printed out, as this was the position before the A. If
this second line of code were now changed to:

```
      ANIMAL @PLACE 'D'
```

3 would become the contents of PLACE, as the third and final
position is where the cursor stopped. PLACE is assigned a value
even though the match failed. If OUTPUT had been used instead of
PLACE:

```
      ANIMAL @OUTPUT 'D'
```

the digits 1, 2, and 3 would have been printed out in a vertical
column because each time the cursor changes position in a
variable, the variable after the @ gets a new value. In this case
the variable is OUTPUT, and each new value is printed out.*

---

*In some complicated matches, the cursor actually moves backwards
in search of characters that will satisfy the pattern sought,
thus the @variable can be used to track the cursor's movement in
either direction.

EXERCISES

1. Pick out the errors in each of the following statements. The
L in LOOP in statement a. defines column 1. If there are no
errors, tell what if anything will be printed. For each statement
assume TEXT contains: ´DO YOU UNDERSTAND CONDITIONAL VALUE
ASSIGNMENT?´

```
a.  LOOP  TEXT  BREAK(?)  . OUTPUT
b.        TEXT  BREAK(?).  OUTPUT
c.        TEXT  BREAK(´ ´) . OUTPUT
d.        TEXT ´A´ BREAK(´?´)   . OUTPUT
e.        TEXT SPAN(´DOY ´) . OUTPUT
f.        TEXT ARB ´?´  . OUTPUT
g         TEXT ´DO´ ARB ´?´  . OUTPUT
h.        TEXT ´DO´ (ARB ´?´)  .  OUTPUT
i.        TEXT (´DO´   ARB ´?´) . OUTPUT
```

Let STRING contain ABCD,1234,EFG,567 at the start of each of
the next 12 exercises. Be sure the programs for each of these
exercises print out the initial and final contents of STRING as
well as any characters matched.

2. Match everything up to the first comma in STRING.

3. Replace everything up to the first comma with NO.COMMA and
replace the comma with a dash.

4. Match the first five characters of STRING.

5. Replace the first five characters with FIVE.

6. Match the first digit in STRING.

7. Match everything after the first comma in STRING.

8. Replace everything after the first comma with BEYOND.

9. Match everything between the first and second commas.

10. Match everything between the first and LAST commas.

11. Replace everything between the first and last commas with
BETWEEN.

12. Delete every other character from STRING starting with the
second character.

13. Reverse the contents of STRING.

14. Write a program which reads in numbers with leading zeros and
prints these numbers without these zeros. Possible numbers might
be 0000027, 034.5, 0023.29, 23.29, 23.2900, and 239000.00.
These numbers should be printed in a vertical list with the decimal points aligned:

```
              27
              34.5
              23.29
              23.29
              23.2900
          239000.00
```

15. Write a program which reads in strings of digits and outputs
them as dollar and cents amounts. Thus 93874295 would result in
$938,742.95. Be sure to have commas separate each group of three
digits.

16. Write a program which inserts the check protect symbol (the
asterisk: *) into dollar amounts up to six figures. For example,
$145.67 would become $***145.67, $23.50 would become $****23.50,
and $213456.00 would remain unchanged.

17. Write a program which changes letter prefix phone numbers
(e.g. PE 6-5000) to all numeric ones (e.g. 736-5000). Use at
least ten different numbers as data.

18. Write a program which changes the normal ordering of a name
(first name   middle name   last name) to last name,   first name
middle name.

19. Write a program which will accept either of the formats
described in Exercise 18 and substitute initials for the first and
middle names.

20.   Assume the following code:

```
LOOK = PATTERN . OUTPUT
'-$983,479.42'  LOOK
```

If PATTERN is assigned each of the following in turn, tell what

the above two lines would print with each assignment.

a.   SPAN(983)
b.   SPAN(98347942)
c.   SPAN(987654321)
d.   SPAN('987654321')
e.   ('-' ARB ',')
f.   '$'
g.   ('$' REM)
h.   ('.' LEN(2))
i.   BREAK('.')
j.   '-'

21.   Assume a string of 100 digits contains several unwanted

letters. Write a program which uses the cursor position operator

(@) to pinpoint their locations.

Chapter 5.
Arithmetic and Functions in SNOBOL

>>> Arithmetic Operations

Arithmetic is possible in SNOBOL. Subtraction (-), multiplica-
tion (*), division (/), and exponentiation (**) as well as addition (+) (which has already been introduced indirectly) are all
easy to do in SNOBOL. The symbols in parentheses after each
operation are the operators used to perform them.

Decimals as well as integers may be used for all operations.
If both types of numbers are used in the same statement, the
result is a decimal number. As has been illustrated in Table 2-1,
a digit may be treated both as a number and as a string of characters to be manipulated. Arithmetic is usually done in the context
of an assign statement. For example:

        TALLY = TALLY + 1

This statement increases the numeric value of TALLY by one. TALLY
has to contain just numbers (or numbers and a decimal point) for
this statement to be executed without error by SNOBOL. Plus or
minus signs are also acceptable as the first character of a numeric variable (such as TALLY).

81

In SNOBOL, numeric variables as well as all other variables are set to zero or null before the execution of a program begins. Thus the SNOBOL programmer does not have to worry about initialization before he uses them.

Below are examples of more arithmetic in SNOBOL:

```
COUNTER = 5 + STEP
TOTAL.COUNT = SUB.COUNT.1 + SUB.COUNT.2 - FUDGE
FINAL.PRODUCT = PART.A * -PART.B
A.POWER = A.NUMBER ** AN.INTEGER
A.FRACTIONAL.RESULT = SOMETHING / 45.2
VARIETY = (3 + XX) * (-4 / YY)
```

Several things should be pointed out about arithmetic in SNOBOL. First, remember that the equals sign should be interpreted as "set equal to" rather than indicating exact equality. Second, any combination of operations is possible. Parentheses can be used freely if there is any doubt as to the sequence in which operations will be performed. Finally, as with almost all SNOBOL operators, spaces must be used in arithmetic computations. At least one blank must be on either side of an arithmetic operator. There are two qualifications to this. Signed numbers should not have a space between the sign and the number, and a parenthesis need have spaces only on its "out-side"--not next to the variable it is enclosing. Table 5-1 shows a variety of arithmetic statements in SNOBOL.

TABLE 5-1.   SNOBOL Arithmetic Statements.

X is assumed empty at the start of each statement.

STATEMENT   CONTENTS OF X

X = 25   25

X = 25.3   25.3

X = X + 1   1

X = X + ´1´   ´1´

X = 7 + 5   12

X = ´24´ / 6   ´4´

X = 24 / 5.0   4.8

X = 24 / 5   4

X = 24.0 / 6   4.0

X = (24 + 2) / 2   13

X = (24 + 2.0) / 2   13.0

X = 23 * 2   46

X = (41 + 5.0) / 2   23.0

X = 0.5 - 2   -1.5

X = 13 ** 2   169

X = (5 ** 2) / 10   2

X = 0.333   .333

X = .333   causes an error because a zero
                  must come before the decimal
                  point in any decimal fractions

>>> Arithmetic Functions

It is possible to make a variety of comparisons between numeric variables. Six functions are provided in SNOBOL which compare numeric variables as to their magnitude:

GE(X,Y) asks if X is greater than or equal to Y.
GT(X,Y) asks if X is greater than Y.
LT(X,Y) asks if X is less than Y.
LE(X,Y) asks if X is less than or equal to Y.
NE(X,Y) asks if X is NOT equal to Y.
EQ(X,Y) asks if X is equal to Y.

Some statements using these functions are:

```
      GT(COUNTER,10)    :S(FINISH.UP)
```

If COUNTER is greater than 10 the program branches to a statement labeled FINISH.UP.

```
      NE(OLD.RESULT,NEW.RESULT)   :S(MISTAKE)F(ALL.OK)
```

If the two RESULTs are not equal it is assumed something is wrong and a branch is taken to MISTAKE. If they are numerically equal the program goes to ALL.OK.

These arithmetic functions are very useful for controlling iterations through a loop (i.e. counting the number of times a set of statements is to be executed). In the following code, GT() is used to read in 8 names--a hypothetical maximum number of students allowed in a seminar.

```
                 OUTPUT = 'SEMINAR STUDENTS:'
      MORE TALLY = TALLY + 1
                 GT(TALLY,8)   :S(END)
                 OUTPUT = INPUT :S(MORE)
      END
```

The next eight cards (or more) would be student names.

One loop can be nested or used inside another. Consider a list
of 22 students who must be assigned to seminars--with a maximum of
8 students per seminar. In this case seminars as well as students
must be counted. The following program and output show how this
can be done. There are 22 data cards for the program--one per
student.

```
      -LIST LEFT
1                            &TRIM = 1
      *
      *
      ******* ADD A SEMINAR ****************************
      *
2     NEXT.SEMINAR   SEMINAR.COUNT = SEMINAR.COUNT + 1
3                    OUTPUT =
4                    OUTPUT = 'SEMINAR ' SEMINAR.COUNT
4     +                     ' STUDENTS:'
5                    STUDENT.COUNT = 0
      *
      *
      ******* READ IN STUDENTS *************************
      *
6     NEXT.STUDENT   STUDENT.COUNT = STUDENT.COUNT + 1
7                    GT(STUDENT.COUNT,8) :S(NEXT.SEMINAR)
8                    OUTPUT = INPUT :S(NEXT.STUDENT)
9     END

SEMINAR 1 STUDENTS:
JOHN
GARY
PAULA
RONALD
DIANNE
KENNETH
JAMES
THOMAS

SEMINAR 2 STUDENTS:
MARK
BARRY
```

```
DAVID
PHILIPPE
LARRY
SCOTT
DANIEL
ANDREW

SEMINAR 3 STUDENTS:
FRED
NEIL
PHOEBE
JEAN
REX
WILLIAM
```

If there is a maximum of two seminars available, an arithmetic function can be used to check SEMINAR.COUNT for this value. This has been done in the following code. The input is the same 22 names as before

```
        -LIST LEFT
1                       &TRIM = 1
        *
        *
        ******* ADD A SEMINAR ********************************
        *
2       NEXT.SEMINAR    SEMINAR.COUNT = SEMINAR.COUNT + 1
3                       OUTPUT =
4                       LE(SEMINAR.COUNT,2) :F(QUOTA.REACHED)
5                       OUTPUT = 'SEMINAR ' SEMINAR.COUNT
5       +                        ' STUDENTS:'
6                       STUDENT.COUNT = 0
        *
        *
        ******* READ IN STUDENTS ***************************
        *
7       NEXT.STUDENT    STUDENT.COUNT = STUDENT.COUNT + 1
8                       GT(STUDENT.COUNT,8) :S(NEXT.SEMINAR)
9                       OUTPUT = INPUT :F(END)S(NEXT.STUDENT)
        *
        *
        ******* NOTE THAT QUOTA IS REACHED ******************
        *
10      QUOTA.REACHED   OUTPUT = 'AVAILABLE SEMINARS ARE FULL.'
11      END

SEMINAR 1 STUDENTS:
JOHN
GARY
PAULA
```

RONALD
DIANNE
KENNETH
JAMES
THOMAS

SEMINAR 2 STUDENTS:
MARK
BARRY
DAVID
PHILIPPE
LARRY
SCOTT
DANIEL
ANDREW

AVAILABLE SEMINARS ARE FULL.

>>> Other Useful SNOBOL Functions

   IDENT(). Besides comparing the numeric contents of variables,
it is possible to look at their literal contents whether numeric
or not. IDENT(object.1,object.2) asks if the two arguments (i.e.
object.1 and object.2)--be they either variables or
literals--CONTAIN exactly the same characters. The characters can
be anything, but for this function to succeed there must be the
same number of characters in each variable or literal and they
must be identical on a character-for-character basis. Using
IDENT():

        IDENT(LIST,´ABCDEFGHIJKLMNOPQRSTUVWXYZ´) :S(PRINT.ABC)
   The variable LIST must contain the literal characters in the
alphabet (and only these characters) for this statement to succeed.

```
        IDENT(LINE,SOUGHT.FOR.LINE)   :S(FOUND.IT)
```

If LINE and SOUGHT.FOR.LINE are identical, the program containing this statement branches to FOUND.IT.

A special use of IDENT() asks if a variable is empty:

```
        IDENT(STRING)   :F(STRING.STILL.HAS.SOMETHING)
```

By omitting one of the arguments, the remaining argument in
IDENT() is compared with the null string. In this statement,
processing would continue with the immediately following statement
if STRING were empty.

LGT(). Alphabetical or "lexical" comparison can be done with
the LGT() or "lexically greater than" function in SNOBOL. This
function which has two arguments asks if the first argument comes
after the second alphabetically. In other words, is the first
argument further along in the alphabet (i.e. lexically greater)
than the second. Some examples:

```
        LET.2 = ´W´
        LGT(LET.1,LET.2)   :S(LET.1.IS.X.Y.OR.Z)
```

The goto here is self-explanatory about the result of this
function.

```
        LGT(SECOND.WORD,FIRST.WORD)
```

This statement will succeed if SECOND.WORD comes after
FIRST.WORD in the dictionary. Though LGT() may seem to be placing
its arguments backwards, a little study will insure its correct
use.

The following program and output illustrate how LGT() can be

used to sort a string of words in alphabetical order. In this
code, a simple "drop-out" technique is used to sort the names of
10 state capitals.*

```
        -LIST LEFT
1           UNSORTED.CAPITALS = 'ST.PAUL, JACKSON, LANSING, '
1       +                      'SANTA FE, TRENTON, RALEIGH, '
1       +                      'ALBANY, CARSON CITY, '
1       +                      'PIERRE, SPRINGFIELD, '
2           OUTPUT = 'SORTED CAPITALS:'
3       SORT CAPITALS = UNSORTED.CAPITALS
        *
        *
        ******* FIND FIRST CAPITAL FROM REMAINING ONES ***********
        *
4           CAPITALS BREAK(',') . CAPITAL ', ' = :F(END)
5       NEXT CAPITALS BREAK(',') . NEW.CAPITAL ', ' = :F(HAVE.ONE)
6           LGT(CAPITAL,NEW.CAPITAL)  :F(NEXT)
7           CAPITAL = NEW.CAPITAL :(NEXT)
        *
        *
        ******* PRINT AND DELETE CAPITAL ************************
        *
8       HAVE.ONE OUTPUT = CAPITAL
9           UNSORTED.CAPITALS CAPITAL ', ' = :(SORT)
10      END
```

```
SORTED CAPITALS:
ALBANY
CARSON CITY
JACKSON
LANSING
PIERRE
RALEIGH
SANTA FE
SPRINGFIELD
ST.PAUL
TRENTON
```

The logic of this sort is to find the alphabetically first
object of those that remain in the list called UNSORTED.CAPITALS.
This is accomplished in statements 4, 5, 6, and 7. Statement 4

---

*There are many methods of sorting, thus for extensive sorting a
programmer is well advised to weigh carefully how efficient each
method will be.

breaks off the initial capital from CAPITALS and stores it in
CAPITAL. In succession, each remaining capital is broken off by
statement 5 and stored in NEW.CAPITAL. Statement 6 checks if
NEW.CAPITAL comes before CAPITAL, and if so statement 7 assigns
CAPITAL the value of NEW.CAPITAL. Finally CAPITALS is exhausted
in statement 5 and the program branches to HAVE.ONE--with CAPITAL
containing the alphabetically first capital from those remaining.

Once this capital is found it is printed (statement 8) and
deleted from the unsorted list (statement 9). The program then
loops back to statement 3 to find the next capital. In effect the
list to be sorted is searched as many times as there are
objects--though each time the search is shortened because there is
one less object.

SIZE(). SIZE() is a very simple, one argument function. The
value it returns is the number of characters in its argument. If
its argument is an empty variable, it returns a value of zero.
SIZE() always succeeds. Some examples of SIZE():

>   TOTAL = 24 + SIZE(ALPHABET)

This would assign 50 to TOTAL if ALPHABET contained its usual
26 letters.

>   SENTENCE = ´THIS IS AN ARGUMENT FOR SIZE()´
>   OUTPUT = SIZE(SENTENCE)

Here 30 would be printed. Note that spaces count as characters
for SIZE().

>>> Functions as a Gate

An assignment can be made conditional on the outcome of a
function: a function can act like a "gate," controlling whether
assignment takes place or not. Here is an example using a function as a gate:

         TALLY = LT(TALLY,10) TALLY + 1 :S(LOOP.AGAIN)

In this statement, TALLY is incremented only if it is less than
10. The LT(TALLY,10) part of this code acts like a gate or valve;
it is open and allows TALLY + 1 to become the contents of TALLY if
TALLY is less than 10. If TALLY is 10 or more, the assignment
does not happen. If a function used as a gate succeeds and
assignment takes place, the statement succeeds, and any success
branch that is present is taken.

         STRING = IDENT(STRING) LT(LINES,100) REST

This use of two gates assigns the contents of REST to STRING
only if STRING is empty and if LINES is less than 100.

In the capital sorting example, a gate could have been used to
combine statements 6 and 7:

         CAPITAL = LGT(CAPITAL,NEW.CAPITAL) NEW.CAPITAL :(NEXT)

CAPITAL gets the value of NEW.CAPITAL if NEW.CAPITAL is alphabetically before CAPITAL. Whether this exchange is made or not, the
program branches to NEXT as before.

EXERCISES

1. If STRING contains various letters and numbers, but definitely
has a digit as its second character, add one to this digit and
store the result back in STRING. Be sure to print out the initial
and final contents of STRING.

2. Write a program which prints out the following five times:
THIS MESSAGE HAS BEEN PRINTED n TIME(S). n should equal 1 the
first time, 2 the second time, etc. Use the gate concept to
control this loop. Try to write this program in two statements.

3. Write a program which uses a gate to control a loop. The loop
should break off the first 10 characters of a 35 character string
and output them individually as they are broken off. Have
SIZE(STRING) be one of the arguments of the function used in the
gate.

4. Write a program which keeps track of transactions for a
checking account. The single string variable ACCOUNT should
contain the current balance, checks which have cleared (serial
number, amount, & date) and deposits which have been credited
(amount and date). Each check or deposit should come on a
separate data card. Print out the account balance after each

transaction. The use of delimiting characters is all important in
this problem; their judicious selection should make this a
relatively easy exercise.

5. Extend the above exercise so that it prints a statement at the
end of each of the three months. Use a special card (e.g. the
month name) to separate one month's transactions from the next.
Be sure to use sufficient test data in order to demonstrate all
the capabilities of this program.

Chapter 6.
User-Defined Functions in SNOBOL

A user frequently may need to use essentially the same set of statements with different arguments again and again. Continually retyping virtually the same code is very boring, not to mention being inefficient. To overcome this inefficiency, SNOBOL allows users to define their own functions. It is possible to program a wide variety of functions including those which do the same things to different strings and those which do different things to the same strings.

For example, a possible function might take a string of characters which are assumed to be words of text separated by blanks and print out this string, breaking each line at a blank rather than in the middle of a word. This function would likely have many uses in any program which handles long passages of text. Further, such a function could be programmed to allow specification of a desired maximum line length.

Using functions also permits modular programming. If each module or part of a program is written as a function, and they are all drawn together as one main program, the logic of this main program is often clearer not only to those not involved with the programming, but also frequently to the programmer(s) as well. Using functions for modular programming is also desirable when

several people work on the same program; each can write a function
or series of functions to do one part of the required program.
Combining such functions to make one main program is almost always
easier than putting together separately written pieces of
code--which invariably employ the same variable names, but for
different tasks.

>>> Parts of a User-Defined Function

A user-defined function in SNOBOL has three parts:

> 1. A definition
>
> 2. A call or use
>
> 3. Actual code

A definition indicates the general form of the function call or
use. It also tells SNOBOL to look for the function code (as well
as a number of details about this code). Function definitions are
usually placed at the beginning of a program to insure that they
are executed, and executed only once.

The actual code which determines what the function does is
usually placed at the end of a program. It is quite important
that the sequence of control in the program which uses the function does not flow into the function code. A programmer must use
a goto to branch around any function code.*

---

*If an attempt is made to execute function code by flowing into
it, an error will be produced because the function will try to
return to where it was called from, but no such spot will exist.

A call or use of a function can occur anywhere in a program
(after the function definition) and as many times as the user
wishes. Figure 6-1 outlines the relationship between these three
parts of a function.

FIGURE 6-1. Function definition, calls, and code.

SNOBOL
program:

```
DEFINE() function

statement
statement
      .
      .
      .
statement
statement

call function

statement
statement
      .
      .
      .
statement
statement

call function

statement
statement
      .
      .
      .
statement
statement    :(END)

code for function

END
```

>>> A Sample Function

The following is an example of the SNOBOL function which has
already been suggested. Briefly, a call of this function prints
out the contents of its first argument (TEXT), never breaking a
line in the middle of a word, and averaging a line length of
approximately the value of its second argument (LL).

First, the function definition:

        DEFINE('PRINT(TEXT,LL)LINE,WORD','PRINT.IT')

Possible uses:

        PRINT(PASSAGE,60)
        PRINT(TEXT,55)
        PRINT(PARAGRAPH,72)

In each of these calls of PRINT(), a variable (PASSAGE, TEXT,
or PARAGRAPH) is assumed to contain textual material consisting of
words separated by blanks. These calls cause this material to be
printed out with no breaking of words over lines. The line
lengths average 60, 55, and 72 spaces respectively.

The actual code for the PRINT() function:

```
PRINT.IT SAVE.ANCHOR = &ANCHOR ; &ANCHOR = 1
*
*
****** DELETE ANY BLANKS FROM REMAINDER OF TEXT *****
*
FRONT.TRIM TEXT ' ' = :S(FRONT.TRIM)
     LINE =
*
*
****** BUILD UP AN OUTPUT LINE *********************
```

```
*
NEXT.WORD TEXT BREAK(´ ´) . WORD ´ ´ =  :F(LAST.LINE)
      LINE = LINE WORD ´ ´
      OUTPUT = GT((SIZE(LINE) + 5),LL) LINE
+:S(FRONT.TRIM)F(NEXT.WORD)
LAST.LINE OUTPUT = LINE TEXT
      &ANCHOR = SAVE.ANCHOR :(RETURN)
```

Even before describing the DEFINE() function, it should be
fairly clear how the code for the PRINT() function works. The
only new thing which has been used in this code is the keyword
&ANCHOR. The assignment of a nonzero value to this keyword alters
pattern matching in a simple way: all matches MUST start with the
first character in a variable. Using &ANCHOR in this function
insures that only INITIAL blanks will be deleted from TEXT.
Without &ANCHOR = 1, blanks between words would also be deleted by
TEXT ´ ´ = . This deletion of blanks is done everytime a new line
is started.

The remainder of this code uses a gate to control the size of
LINE. When LINE is within 5 characters of LL, it is printed out
and a new line is started. The reason for this use of LL - 5 is
that as words get added to LINE, SIZE(LINE) may jump from under LL
to over LL. By checking five spaces before LL is reached, this
function insures that the length of an average line will not
continually exceed LL. The value 5 was chosen because it is
approximately the length of an average word.

When no more words can be broken off of TEXT, transfer is made
to LAST.LINE which outputs the partial line created so far and the
residual in TEXT. There will usually be something left in TEXT
because TEXT typically will not end with a blank; hence, it will
not be possible to break off the last word. The final line of the

function code restores the value of &ANCHOR. Saving and restoring
the value of this keyword guarantees that the main program will
not be affected by the use of this keyword. This final line of
the function goes back to the main program via the special RETURN
goto which is required of all functions. (More details about this
goto will be presented shortly.)

>>> The DEFINE() Function

The general form of the DEFINE() function is:

```
DEFINE('name(argument(s))local.variable(s)','entry.label')
```

This definition tells SNOBOL what the function call looks like,
what variables are "local" to the function, and what the starting
statement or "entry label" is. Consider below the sample function
which has just been illustrated:

FUNCTION PROTOTYPE. The prototype of this function is
PRINT(TEXT,LL). Within the function, TEXT and LL are respectively
assigned the values of the two arguments used in the call of this
function (e.g. PASSAGE and 60). It is important to realize that
arguments for a user-defined function are local to the
function--that is if these names are used for other purposes
elsewhere in the program, calling the function will not change
their values. Thus, this user-defined function is quite similar
to existing functions in SNOBOL. It simply causes some processing
when it is called or "referred to".

LOCAL VARIABLES. The local variables for the PRINT() function
are LINE and WORD. What is meant here is the same as the
reference to local with regard to a function's arguments. These
two variables have a special use within the function which is
LOCAL to the function; they may have entirely different uses in
the program outside the function. This specifying of local
variables relieves the user from the responsibility of saving
values if he has used these names elsewhere in the program (or in
fact of even remembering if he has), for even if he has, the
function's use of them will not disturb their original values.

If variables used in a function are not defined as local (with
the exception of a function's arguments), they can be used by the
main program (the code outside the function) or the function
itself. In other words, either is free to change these variables'
values and either must accept the values left to it by the other.
If a function changes the contents of a nonlocal variable from
what the main program had assigned to it, the main program will
find this change when the flow of control returns from the function. If the variable was local, SNOBOL would restore the value
the main program had given the variable before returning control
to the main program. Hence, a main program will never find a
function causing unwanted side-effects by changing the values of
any of its variables if they are declared local to the function.

It is legitimate and often useful to have a function CHANGE
nonlocal variables. For example the following function
INITIALIZE() might be used to assign predetermined values to a

number of nonlocal variables so a given loop or process could be
executed again.

The definition:

```
DEFINE('INITIALIZE()','START')
```

The call:

```
INITIALIZE()
```

The code:

```
START CLOCK = 1
      ERRORS = 0
      LIMIT = 10
      TRIAL.COUNTER = 0
      RESPONSES =    :(RETURN)
```

This function has no argument at all; this is not necessary for a
function which changes global variables, however.

FUNCTION ENTRY LABEL. The meaning of the entry label is
straight-forward. This label is the point to which control is
transferred when a function is called. A short cut in function
definition is frequently employed which uses an implied entry
point. The function name (e.g. PRINT) can be used as the label
for the first line of function code and transfer of control from a
function call occurs automatically to this point. If this change
were made in the PRINT() function, the definition for this function would become:

```
DEFINE('PRINT(TEXT,LL)LINE,WORD')
```

This would also imply that the label PRINT.IT would have to be
changed to PRINT because an explicit entry label is not given. It
is important to keep in mind that labels in a SNOBOL program are

global to the entire program.   They cannot be made local as can
variables.   This means that no label can be used more than
once--whether it is in a function or not.

>>> Returning from a Function

    Implied in the fact that a function is called by a main program
is the necessity for the function to be able to return the flow of
control to the point of call.   This is done using a special goto:

> :(RETURN)

Return to the main program can also be conditional:

> :S(RETURN)   or   :F(RETURN)

As is the case with IDENT(), LT(), GT(), etc., a user-defined
function can succeed or fail.   This is accomplished through the
use of an additional return goto:

> :(FRETURN)   or   :S(FRETURN)   or   :F(FRETURN)

The F in FRETURN stands for failure.   If a function returns to a
main program via the FRETURN goto, the statement which called the
function fails.   This does not mean that the function did not
accomplish something or that other processing in the call was not
carried out, but that if the call statement has a conditional
goto, it will take the failure branch.   For example, the PRINT()
function could be changed to fail if TEXT were empty.   Thus the
flow of control could be changed if nothing was printed.

>>> Functions Which Return a Value

As with functions such as SIZE(), user-defined functions can
also return values. The function name is treated as a variable
within the function, and the value the function is to return is
assigned to this name. COUNT() is an example of such a function:

```
COUNT IDENT(LIST)   :S(FRETURN)
      COUNT = 0
***** THIS FUNCTION ASSUMES NO MULTIPLE
***** DELIMITERS BETWEEN LIST MEMBERS.
NEXT LIST DELIMITER = :F(RETURN)
      COUNT = COUNT + 1   :(NEXT)
```

COUNT() returns as its value the number of "items" in a string.
Such a string might be made up of a list of words where each word
is followed by a delimiter such as a slash. COUNT() assumes a
single delimiter after every item. This function fails if LIST is
empty (i.e. the first statement takes the FRETURN branch). Though
COUNT() deletes delimiters within its actual code, the arguments
it is called with are unchanged upon its return (i.e. the variable
in LIST's position in the call still contains delimiters). The
following statement would define COUNT():

```
DEFINE('COUNT(LIST,DELIMITER)')
```

Uses for COUNT() might include:

```
TOTAL = COUNT(OLD.LIST,' ') + COUNT(NEW.LIST,'/')
```

Here TOTAL would contain the number of items in both lists.

```
  AVERAGE.SIZE = (SIZE(STRING) - COUNT(STRING,',')) /
+ COUNT(STRING,',')
```

In this example, the number of characters in STRING is determined, the number of delimiters subtracted (as this is the same as
the number of items), and the result divided by the number of
items to obtain the average length of a list member. This code
could be made much more efficient with respect to computer time if
items were counted only once:

```
      N.ITEMS = COUNT(STRING,´,´)
      AVERAGE.SIZE = (SIZE(STRING) - N.ITEMS) / N.ITEMS
```

Here the number of items is saved as N.ITEMS and used both
places where COUNT(STRING,´,´) was used.

Frequently it is useful to have random numbers available in a
SNOBOL program. The following short function* returns a
pseudo-random integer from 1 through N each time is is called.
These integers are distributed uniformly as the sample output
shows.

```
         -LIST LEFT
1            &TRIM = 1
         *
         *
         ****** FUNCTION DEFINITION *****************************
         *
2            DEFINE(´RANDOM(N)´)    :(USE)
         *
         *
         ****** FUNCTION CODE **********************************
         *
3        RANDOM SEED = SEED * 1061 + 3251
4            (SEED ´/´) LEN(5) . SEED ´/´
```

---

*This function has been adapted from: R. E. Griswold, J. F.
Poage, & I. P. Polonsky, THE SNOBOL4 PROGRAMMING LANGUAGE,
Prentice-Hall, Englewood Cliffs (N.J.), 1968, p. 89.

```
5           RANDOM = ((SEED * N) / 100000) + 1 :(RETURN)
    *
    *
    ****** FUNCTION USE **************************************
    *
6    USE OUTPUT = 'RANDOM NUMBERS? (Y/N)'
7        ANSWER = INPUT ;   IDENT(ANSWER,'Y')   :F(END)
9        COUNT = 0
10       OUTPUT = 'SEED?'   ;  SEED = INPUT
12       OUTPUT = 'TOP OF RANGE?'   ;  N = INPUT
14       OUTPUT = 'HOW MANY NUMBERS?'   ;  AMOUNT = INPUT
16   MORE COUNT = COUNT + 1
17       LINE = LE(COUNT,AMOUNT) LINE ' ' RANDOM(N) :S(MORE)
18       OUTPUT = LINE  ;  LINE =   :(USE)
20   END
```

```
RANDOM NUMBERS? (Y/N)
>Y
SEED?
>37
TOP OF RANGE?
>2
HOW MANY NUMBERS?
>20
   1 1 1 2 1 2 2 1 2 1 1 1 2 2 2 2 1 1 2 1 2
RANDOM NUMBERS? (Y/N)
>Y
SEED?
>7
TOP OF RANGE?
>5
HOW MANY NUMBERS?
>20
   1 2 1 5 4 3 4 4 5 4 1 3 3 5 4 3 5 1 3 5
RANDOM NUMBERS? (Y/N)
>Y
SEED?
>31
TOP OF RANGE?
>1000
HOW MANY NUMBERS?
>10
   362 500 610 649 932 736 897 410 32 879
RANDOM NUMBERS? (Y/N)
>N
```

In addition to illustrating the random number function, this
example shows the "interactive" use of SNOBOL. For those computers on which it is possible, this is a very powerful way to use

SNOBOL. Essentially it is as if the user has the whole computer totally devoted to his needs alone; as soon as he types something at a teletypewriter, he receives an answer. In reality, the computer only gives him a small slice of time and handles other users while he is typing or thinking--hence interactive computing is often called timesharing.

In this example, the user has previously entered the program and has stored it on a file. The input he supplies occurs on those lines containing the ">" symbol.

This program also shows an interesting construction in statement 4. Here a variable (SEED) and a literal (/) are concatenated as the subject of a pattern match. This insures that the conditional assignment of five characters to SEED will take the LAST five (i.e. those before the slash).

A final point about this function is that SEED is not local and hence its value is carried from one call to another--unless it is changed by the calling program. INPUT changes it in this example.

EXERCISES

1. Write a function which returns as its value the reversed
contents of a string. The initial string is not to be changed.
(Hint: this code has already been given but not as a function.)

2. Write a function which returns as its value a sentence with
all of its vowels replaced by dashes.

3. Write a function which sorts a string of words in alphabetical
order. The value the function returns should be the sorted
string. To make the function as general as possible, it should
have three arguments: the name of the string to be sorted, the
character which delimits the words, and the direction of sort
desired (A to Z or Z to A). Be sure to use an appropriate variety
of test runs and data to check the program's correctness.

4. Randomly select five DIFFERENT words from a paragraph of
unknown length which is read in as data. Both the initial paragraph and the words selected should be printed. The selection
procedure should NOT delete the words from the paragraph.

Chapter 7.
Indirect Reference

Indirect reference is a powerful technique which is very useful in SNOBOL. The idea behind indirect reference is quite simple: the literal characters in a variable (often concatenated with other literals) are treated as the name of another variable or as a label within a goto. Figure 7-1 shows this schematically.

FIGURE 7-1. Indirect reference.

Assume:

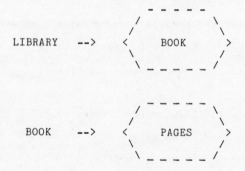

Then:

$LIBRARY   -->   <   PAGES   >

The dollar sign ($) is used as the operator for indirect
reference.* Placing the $ before LIBRARY causes SNOBOL to look
within LIBRARY for a name rather than treating LIBRARY itself as
the name. This indirect referencing generates BOOK which is then
considered the name to be used; hence, $LIBRARY contains PAGES.
The actual code for this would be:

```
BOOK = ´PAGES´
LIBRARY = ´BOOK´
OUTPUT = $LIBRARY
```

These three statements would cause PAGES to be printed. The
sections which follow show examples of this technique as well as
other uses for indirect reference.

>>> Using Indirect Reference To Store Attributes

Indirect reference gives the SNOBOL programmer the capability
to store a characteristic or attribute of a string of characters
in the variable whose name is the characters themselves. For

---

*This operator is called a "unary" operator because there is a
space only to its left, rather than on both sides as with binary
operators (e.g. the equals sign and the period used for conditional value assignment).

example the length of a word could be computed and stored as the
contents of the word:

```
     WORD = ´SERENDIPITY´
     $WORD = SIZE(WORD)
```

These two statements accomplish the assignment of 11 to the
variable called SERENDIPITY. It is just as if SERENDIPITY = 11
had been used. The following statements store a person´s age and
sex as the value of his name:

```
     NAME = ´RALPH´
     $NAME = ´MALE,47´
```

RALPH now contains MALE,47. Multiple levels of indirect reference
are possible. Names for the fields charaterizing RALPH could have
been introduced this way:

```
     NAME = ´RALPH´ ; AGE.AND.SEX = ´MALE,47´
     $NAME = ´AGE.AND.SEX´
     OUTPUT = $$NAME
```

Here MALE,47 would be printed out. Multiple level indirect
referencing could also involve hierarchical storage or pyramiding
of word meanings:

```
     SENTENCE = ´JOHN IS A BOY ´
     JOHN = ´SON´
     IS = ´EQUALS´
     A = ´ARTICLE´
     BOY = ´YOUNGSTER´
     SON = ´OFFSPRING´
     EQUALS = ´SAME´
     SAME = ´EQUALITY´
     ARTICLE = ´POINTER´
NEXT.WORD SENTENCE BREAK(´ ´) . WORD ´ ´ = :F(END.DEF)
MORE OUTPUT = DIFFER($WORD) WORD ´ MEANS ´ $WORD
+ :F(NEXT.WORD)
     WORD = $WORD  :(MORE)
END.DEF OUTPUT = ´END OF DEFINITION´
```

This code suggests how the meanings of words can be stored in the words themselves--as many levels deep as desired. This code prints out all of the definitions of all of the words it "knows". Knowing the definition of a word means that $WORD contains something (i.e it is DIFFERent from null).* The looping in the last four lines of the previous code would cause the following list to be printed:

```
JOHN MEANS SON
SON MEANS OFFSPRING
IS MEANS EQUALS
EQUALS MEANS SAME
SAME MEANS EQUALITY
A MEANS ARTICLE
ARTICLE MEANS POINTER
BOY MEANS YOUNGSTER
END OF DEFINITION
```

Using indirect reference to store a word's meaning can easily be extended to handle multiple word definitions. It should be obvious, though, that output would soon mushroom if the meanings of all words in all definitions were traced. This points up one of the difficulties encountered in semantic analysis; context must be considered not only to define meaning but to limit it as well.

>>> Referencing Labels Indirectly

Indirect reference can be used to store a label in a goto, rather than a name in a variable. This is useful because it

---

*DIFFER() is a function which is the exact opposite of IDENT(); it succeeds if its two arguments are at all different from one another. Defaulting one argument causes the remaining one to be compared with null.

allows a program to compute where it will go next while it is
running rather than being restricted to a binary choice as is the
case in an ordinary conditional goto. This use of indirect
reference is therefore sometimes called a "computed goto".
Consider the next example which takes various branches based on a
person´s credit rating:

```
      &TRIM = 1
NEXT  RATING = INPUT :S($RATING)F(END)
EXCELLENT OUTPUT = ´CREDIT LIMIT IS $2000´   :(NEXT)
GOOD      OUTPUT = ´CREDIT LIMIT IS $1000´   :(NEXT)
FAIR      OUTPUT = ´CREDIT LIMIT IS $500´    :(NEXT)
POOR      OUTPUT = ´CREDIT LIMIT IS $100´    :(NEXT)
BAD.RISK  OUTPUT = ´PLEASE RETURN YOUR CREDIT CARD´   :(NEXT)
END
```

This program prints out one of five messages based on the contents
of an input card (which is assumed to contain EXCELLENT, GOOD,
FAIR, POOR, or BAD.RISK). Of course the card can contain other
input information as it probably would if this were a real
business program, and this kind of code could still be used as
long as the proper field in the input card was matched and
assigned to RATING.

Another example of a label using indirect reference is:

```
    PROCESS.SEQUENCE = ´PROC.1,PROC.23,PROC.47,PROC.9,´
RETURN.HERE PROCESS.SEQUENCE BREAK(´,´) . PROCESS ´,´ =
+   :S($PROCESS)F(DONE)
```

This group of statements can branch to a series of labels. Each
label is broken off of PROCESS.SEQUENCE and a branch is made to
this label by going to the statement whose label is the contents
of PROCESS. The program which contains this code is assumed to
have sections labeled PROC.1, PROC.23, PROC.47, and PROC.9 though

they are not indicated here. It is probable--but not
necessary--that each PROC has a goto that branches back to
RETURN.HERE.*

>>> Concatenation To Achieve Indirect Reference

   If there is a series of variables that are to be treated sequentially or in any definable order (numerical or otherwise),
they can be referenced using the $ operator. Assume the contents
of a number of messages (e.g. MESSAGE.1, MESSAGE.2, MESSAGE.3,
etc.) are to be printed out, code can be set up to do this as
follows:

```
      MORE N = LT(N,5) N + 1 :F(MESSAGES.DONE)
           OUTPUT = ´MESSAGE.´ N ´ IS ´ $(´MESSAGE.´ N)  :(MORE)
```

The heart of this code is $(´MESSAGE.´ N). The literal characters
MESSAGE. are concatenated with the value of N. The result of this
concatenation the first time this code is executed is MESSAGE.1.
The $ around the parentheses then causes these characters to be
treated as a name whose contents are required. Hence, if
MESSAGE.1 contained HI, I CAME FROM A SNOBOL PROGRAM, the first
line of output from this code would be:

   MESSAGE.1 IS HI, I CAME FROM A SNOBOL PROGRAM

Note that MESSAGE.1 IS which is the preface to this message had

---

*Indirect reference must be used to refer to statements which have
 a label that starts with a number. For example, to branch to 88A
 requires :($´88A´) rather than just :(88A).

nothing to do with the indirect reference; it resulted simply from
concatenation of a literal (MESSAGE.), a numeric variable (N), and
another literal (IS).

Concatenation and indirect reference can also be used in a
goto. For example, :($('SPOT' NUM)) would cause a branch to
SPOT23, SPOT47, or SPOT53A if NUM were respectively assigned 23,
47, or 53A.

EXERCISES

1. Set up a program with five ZOOs (ZOO.1, ZOO.2, etc.) each one
of which has four or five animals in it. Write code which then
reads in pairs of data cards. The first data card specifies a ZOO
number, the second an animal. The program should determine if the
selected ZOO contains the given animal. Have the program handle
at least three such pairs of cards printing out appropriate
messages based on success or failure.

2. Write a program which uses indirect reference to store the
capital of a state as the contents of the state name. The initial
state-capital pairs should come in as input data, and in no case
should any actual state or capital names appear in the program.
The program should then accept state names as input and produce
correct capitals as output. If possible, run this program
interactively. (So as to maximize the learning in this exercise,

select states whose capitals you have forgotten and have to look up.)

3. Rewrite the above program so that a capital's population is stored as the contents of its name. The program should accept state or capital names as input and produce the correct capital or population as output.

4. Rewrite Exercise 5 in Chapter 5 to handle more than one account. All information for an account should be stored as the contents of the account holder's name.

5. Write a SNOBOL program which will generate a simple concordance from the sentences you are now reading. The output from this program should provide a vertical list of all unique words in this paragraph with their frequency of occurrence noted after each word. You need not worry about context.

   The program should be able to handle the period at the end of a sentence, the double space after such a period, common punctuation, and a variable number of words per input line. Also be sure the following quote is included as part of this input paragraph: "Of, of, of, of, of, of, of, of, of; there I said 'of' nine times."

6. Revise the above program so it will list the words in alphabetical order. Use the LGT() function.

Chapter 8.
Error Correction:
The Art of Debugging a Program

The best way to handle errors is not to make them to begin
with. A programmer who carefully considers how to put a program
together--often using a flow chart or a more informal
diagram--will make fewer errors than a programmer who just sits
down and starts writing code. Few people can organize the entire
logic of a nontrivial program in their heads without committing
anything to paper.

Structuring a program implies identification of the components
of the problem to be solved. Usually a "top-down" approach works
best: major tasks or segments of processing are defined before
any coding is attempted. In large problems, several levels of
subdivision may be necessary before programmable-size chunks
emerge. When this stage is reached, the functioning of each
component should be clear (i.e. it should be apparent how the code
should be written).

For example, a program which plays bridge might be broken into
the following parts: deal the cards, sort a hand, generate a bid
from a hand given other bids, select a card to play, determine the
winner of a trick, keep score, and so forth. The logic of each of
these components should be quite clear. If it isn't, further
subdivision is in order. In this example, bidding and playing

quite probably need further subdivision--before they are readily programmable.

Care should also be taken to consider the interaction of the components. For example, the bridge program would require that the hand sorting code "know" where to find the hands which were previously dealt so they could be sorted.

Even with careful structuring, few programs run perfectly the first time. It usually takes from 5 to 20 tries for a student to get a medium-level SNOBOL exercise to work right. Semester projects frequently require more than 30 runs. Professional projects or research efforts often require more. Keypunching or typing mistakes (even just one) can cause an error termination. Logical mistakes (i.e. incomplete understanding of the language or the problem) usually are present. As the learning simulation example (in Chapter 1) indicated, forcing an idea into a running program causes that idea to be clarified and often modified.

Given that errors cannot be avoided, how can they be detected and corrected? Typing and keypunch errors usually become obvious after the first run. Logic errors are harder to find.

There are two major aids to help a programmer "debug" a program and isolate the logic errors in it. The first of these is the dump which has already been mentioned. If the keyword &DUMP has a nonzero value when execution is completed, the contents or structure of all variables in the program will be indicated on the printed output. If a variable happens to be empty even though it may have been used, its name will not appear in the dump listing.

Further, any variable which contains a pattern will only have
PATTERN printed as its contents; it is left to the programmer to
determine what this pattern is.

>>> Tracing

A second method of debugging is tracing. As this name implies,
the actions of a program can be monitored or "traced" as the
program is being executed. Such tracing in no way affects what a
program does.

Both branching in a program and changes in variables´ contents
can be followed using tracing. This is particularly useful when a
problem area in a program has been bypassed before the program
terminates, and relevant contents are not indicated in a dump
because they have been changed by a later section of the program.

Tracing is permitted or "turned on" when the keyword &TRACE is
given a positive integer value (e.g. &TRACE = 100). This integer
is the total number of times branching actions or value changes
will be traced.

TRACING BY VALUE. There are two common kinds of tracing.
Tracing by value is generally the most helpful. Value tracing
means that if a variable´s value is being traced, each time its
contents are changed the result will be printed out. The number
of times this change will be traced and printed is limited by the
value of &TRACE. Tracing by value is set up using the TRACE()
function:

```
TRACE('variable','VALUE')
```

The characters ,'VALUE' are optional as value tracing is the
default type of tracing. The following three statements would
cause tracing of the first 150 changes in WORD and LINE:

```
        &TRACE = 150
        TRACE('WORD')
        TRACE('LINE')
```

Note that the variable name is enclosed in quotes. A total of 150
changes will be traced in these two variables. This number need
not be divided equally, e.g., 140-10, 75-75, 0-150, 80-70, and
23-127 are all possible splits. Also it is possible that the full
150 tracings may not be made because there are fewer than 150
changes in these two variables.

TRACING BY LABEL. The second kind of tracing is by label:

```
    TRACE('label','LABEL')
```

This causes a message to be printed which indicates every time a
branch is taken to the given label. No note is made of the
labeled line if it is just flowed into, however. An example of
label tracing is:

```
        &TRACE = 10
        TRACE('NEXT.CARD','LABEL')
```

These two lines would indicate the first ten transfers to the line
labeled NEXT.CARD. A transfer is indicated by noting the statement number from which control was transferred.

Tracing may be turned off at any time by setting &TRACE to

zero.   Value and label tracing may both be used in the same program.

EFFICIENT TRACING.   Tracing can be very useful; it can also be
overwhelming if not used judiciously.   It is very easy to generate
50 pages of output tracing an unending loop.   It is also easy to
trace so many variables and labels that the output is very difficult to follow.   Efficient tracing practice typically does not
require the tracing of more than three variables and two labels.
Setting &TRACE to 100 usually suffices.   This trace output, which
shouldn't exceed two pages, is usually adequate to determine what
unexpected things the program is or is not doing.

If tracing is used intermittently in the course of developing a
program, it does no harm to leave TRACE('variable','VALUE') and
TRACE('label','LABEL') cards in as no tracing will be done unless
&TRACE is an integer greater than zero.

Figure 8-1 shows an actual listing where tracing is used.

FIGURE 8-1.   A listing with tracing.

```
     -LIST LEFT
     *    THE FOLLOWING LISTING INDICATES
     *    THE VARIOUS ASPECTS OF TRACING.
1         &TRACE = 15
2         TRACE('TEXT')
3         TRACE('MORE','LABEL')
4         TEXT = 'THIS CODE TALLIES THE VOWELS IN THIS SENTENCE'
5         OUTPUT = TEXT
6    MORE TEXT ('A' ! 'E' ! 'I' ! 'O' ! 'U') = = :F(PRINT)
7         VOWEL.TALLY = VOWEL.TALLY + 1 :(MORE)
8    PRINT OUTPUT = 'THE ABOVE SENTENCE HAS ' VOWEL.TALLY
8    +    ' VOWELS.'
9    END

    STMNT 4: TEXT = 'THIS CODE TALLIES THE VOWELS IN THIS SENTENCE'
THIS CODE TALLIES THE VOWELS IN THIS SENTENCE
    STMNT 6: TEXT = 'THS CODE TALLIES THE VOWELS IN THIS SENTENCE'
    STMNT 7: TRANSFER TO MORE
    STMNT 6: TEXT = 'THS CDE TALLIES THE VOWELS IN THIS SENTENCE'
    STMNT 7: TRANSFER TO MORE
    STMNT 6: TEXT = 'THS CD TALLIES THE VOWELS IN THIS SENTENCE'
    STMNT 7: TRANSFER TO MORE
    STMNT 6: TEXT = 'THS CD TLLIES THE VOWELS IN THIS SENTENCE'
    STMNT 7: TRANSFER TO MORE
    STMNT 6: TEXT = 'THS CD TLLES THE VOWELS IN THIS SENTENCE'
    STMNT 7: TRANSFER TO MORE
    STMNT 6: TEXT = 'THS CD TLLS THE VOWELS IN THIS SENTENCE'
    STMNT 7: TRANSFER TO MORE
    STMNT 6: TEXT = 'THS CD TLLS TH VOWELS IN THIS SENTENCE'
    STMNT 7: TRANSFER TO MORE
THE ABOVE SENTENCE HAS 14 VOWELS.
```

The program in Figure 8-1 uses a simple alternation pattern to count and delete all of the vowels from a sentence (TEXT). The changes in TEXT are traced as the deletions occur. From the initial assignment of something to TEXT in statement 4, through the seventh deletion, each change is printed. Along with this value tracing is the use of label tracing. The first seven transfers to the statement labeled MORE are recorded. These seven indications of branching, the seven changes in TEXT, and its initial assignment of a value total the 15 traces which were requested in the first statement (&TRACE = 15). Note that more changes are indeed made to delete all 14 vowels but that only the first seven have been traced.

As can be seen, traced output occurs interspersed with regular output; this is somewhat confusing until it is realized that all of the output is printed in the exact sequence in which it was generated. For example, the message THIS CODE TALLIES THE VOWELS IN THIS SENTENCE is printed between two tracings: one that occurred before it in the program and one that occurred after it.

>>> Common Errors

Reading about the following types of errors (which the author has found to be the most common in student programs) may be an additional aid to the beginning programmer.

SYNTAX ERRORS. These are grammatical errors of putting a statement together incorrectly (due either to typing mistakes or to misunderstanding SNOBOL).

1.   Quotes not closed.

     Sample line: WORD = ´MISTAKEN
     SNOBOL Error message: *** UNCLOSED LITERAL

2.   Missing blank on either side of the assign operator (=)
     or the conditional value assignment operator (.).
     Correct usage dictates at least one blank on either side
     of these operators.

     Sample line: WORD= ´MISTAKE´
     SNOBOL Error message: *** ILLEGAL CHARACTER IN ELEMENT
     Sometimes SNOBOL produces an apostrophe which points
     to the approximate location of the error.

3.   Illegal space.

     Sample line: WORD BREAK (´,´) . OUTPUT
     No error message is printed here because SNOBOL considers
     BREAK as just another variable, for it is not IMMEDIATELY
     followed by a parenthesis. All that would be printed by
     this code is a single comma because this is the only thing
     which would have been assigned to OUTPUT.

4.   Code extending beyond column 72. This may be a very hard
     error to detect because a message will be printed only if
     the code inside column 72 has an error due to its being
     incomplete. A useful strategy here is to have a comment
     line composed of 72 asterisks and compare any suspicious
     lines to see if they extend beyond column 72.

LOGIC ERRORS. Logic errors are often due to an imprecise
realization of exactly what processing will take place. The
following mistakes are frequently made by students:

1.   A variable being empty when it is not expected to be.
     Typically, an earlier assign statement may have been
     branched around. The dump should be checked to see if a
     suspect variable is listed; if not, it had no contents at
     the end of the program.

2.   No delimiter at the end of a string. This can cause
     problems when the last item on the string must be broken
     off using a delimiter.

3. Deleting an object from a string without removing its
    delimiter. This mistake causes future attempts at
    BREAK()ing off objects to succeed but with only a null
    assignment to the variable after the conditional value
    assignment operator. This occurs because the delimiting
    character is now the initial character of the string, and
    since everything before it is null, this is what BREAK()
    matches.

4. Mixing up the placement of INPUT and OUTPUT relative to
    the equals sign. The correct format for common applica-
    tions is:

            OUTPUT = something   or
            something = INPUT

5. Failing to realize the difference in precedence in a match
    statement between the assignment operator (=) and the
    conditional value assignment operator (.). The equals
    sign refers to EVERYTHING between itself and the first
    variable or literal in the statement. The period, on the
    other hand, only refers back to the pattern or variable
    immediately before itself. Parentheses can be used to
    group items together so that two or more of them can be
    assigned to a variable (via .) in a match which uses
    conditional value assignment.

6. The error message "TWO CONSECUTIVE I/O FAILURES" can be
    due to either a syntax error or a logic mistake. Not
    having END start in column one on the last program card
    causes this message as does requesting input after a
    request for input has already failed.

7. Asking if a variable is empty via a match statement:

        VAR ´´ :S(NULL)

    This statement will ALWAYS succeed no matter what VAR
    contains. This is true because all variables contain at
    least nothing! Correct usage is:

        IDENT(VAR,´´) :S(NULL)   or   IDENT(VAR) :S(NULL)

EXERCISES

1. Take an existing program which runs correctly and use TRACE()
to print the first 25 changes in a significant variable.

2. Take an existing program which runs correctly and use TRACE()
to follow the first 25 transfers to an important label.

3. Devise code which would cause a program to produce a dump only
if an error is encountered while the program is running.   (Hint:
Setting and resetting &DUMP is involved.)

4. Using a variable rather than a literal as the argument for
TRACE(), revise an existing program so that it reads in as data
the names of the variables to be traced.   The value of &TRACE
should also be read in as data.

Appendices

APPENDIX 1: Keywords and Control Words

KEYWORD   KEYWORD FUNCTION

&ABEND = 0   A nonzero value causes a computer memory
                    dump following program termination (usually
                    installation dependent).

&ANCHOR = 0   A nonzero value specifies that any matching
                    in a variable must start from or be
                    "anchored" at the first character in that
                    variable. See also page 98.

&CODE = 0   Contains run completion code; installation
                    dependent.

&DUMP = 0   A nonzero value causes printing of the
                    contents of all nonempty variables at
                    program termination. See also page 42.

&ERRLIMIT = 0   Specifies number of nonfatal execution
                        errors allowed before termination of execu-
                        tion.

&FTRACE = 0   A nonzero value allows tracing of function
                        calls and returns if a
                        TRACE('function.name','FUNCTION') statement
                        has been executed.

&FULLSCAN = 0   A nonzero value expands matching to look at
                        impossible alternatives, so the course of
                        scanning in a match can be more fully
                        studied by the programmer.

&INPUT = 1   A zero value causes no input to occur.

&MAXLNGTH = 5000   Number of characters allowed in a variable;
                        can be increased if user wishes.

&OUTPUT = 1   A zero value cause no output to occur.

&STATISTICS = 0   A nonzero value causes printing of run
                        statistics such as number of statements
                        executed and amounts of time used (UNIVAC
                        implementation only).

&STLIMIT = 50000   Number of statements which can be executed;
                        can be increased or decreased as the user
                        wishes. See also page 42.

&TIMELIMIT   Set to 5000 milliseconds (5 seconds) less than the run card time limit to allow for a dump if time is running out. May be decreased within a program to prohibit a prior run in a sequence of runs from using all the time allocated to the whole sequence (UNIVAC implementation only).

&TRACE = 0   A nonzero value specifies the number of tracings to be allowed. See also page 118.

&TRIM = 0   A nonzero value causes trailing blanks to be trimmed from input lines. See also page 41.

All of the above unprotected keywords can be changed in the course of a program as the user wishes. Keyword value assignment is just like a typical assign statement; hence, keywords (and their ampersands) are never placed in column one.

CONTROL WORD	CONTROL WORD FUNCTION
-EJECT	Program LISTING (not output) is broken and continued on the top of the next sheet of paper.
-LIST	Program statements are listed from this point on. Statement numbers are placed on the right. This setting is assumed by SNOBOL if the program specifies nothing else.
-LIST LEFT	List program statements with statement numbers on the left. This is particularly useful when output is being printed at a teletypewriter.
-UNLIST	Program listing is suppressed.

Control words with their initial dash must start in column one. There is no limit to the arrangement and number of times different control words can be used in a given program.

APPENDIX 2: More Patterns, Functions, and Operators

The advanced programmer is advised to consult Griswold et al.
(already cited on page 104) for a more complete description of
these patterns, functions, and operators.

PATTERN/FUNCTION   MATCH/VALUE/OPERATION

ABORT   Matches nothing and causes immediate failure
                              of the match; no other alternatives are
                              tried.

ANY(´character(s)´) Matches the first character in a variable
                              that is identical to any of the
                              ´character(s)´.*

APPLY(function.name,argument(s))
                              Returns the value of the function; allows
                              calling different functions based on the
                              value assigned to function.name and
                              argument(s).

---

*Any reference to ´character(s)´ in this Appendix can be replaced
with a variable name as long as the variable has appropriate
contents. When literal characters are referred to this way, they
must be enclosed in quotes.

ARB   See page 61.

ARBNO('character(s)')

                        Matches as many entire groups of characters as necessary to make the rest of the match succeed. ARBNO() may also have a datatype as its argument.

ARG(function.name,n) Returns the name of the nth argument of a function.

ARRAY()   See page 139.

BACKSPACE()   Data file handling; installation dependent.

BAL   Matches the first string encountered in a variable which has balanced parentheses; absence of parentheses is considered a balance.

BREAK('character(s)')   See page 54.

CLEAR()   Nulls the value of all user-created variables in a program.

CODE('character(s)') Compiles 'character(s)' into Polish prefix SNOBOL object code which can be executed as a program is running.

COLLECT(n)   Fails if less than n bytes of storage re-main; COLLECT() (with no argument) causes a

regeneration of dynamic storage ("garbage
collection") and returns as its value the
number of bytes of storage availabe.

CONVERT(object,´datatype´)

Converts an object to the kind of
datatype specified (i.e. INTEGER, ARRAY,
etc.).

COPY(datatype.object)

A copy of the datatype.object is
returned. Only tables cannot be copied.

DATA()   See page 141.

DATATYPE(object)   Returns the datatype of object (i.e. ARRAY,
                      TABLE, INTEGER, etc.).

DATE()   Returns the current date in slash format:
                      12/25/74.

DEFINE()   See page 99.

DETACH(´name´)   Removes any input or output function of a
                      name.

DIFFER(variable.1,variable.2)   See Page 111.

DUMP(n)   Prints a dump anytime during execution if n
                      is a positive nonzero integer.

DUPL(´character(s)´,n)

Returns ´character(s)´ duplicated n times.

ENDFILE()   Data file handling; installation dependent.

EQ(x,y)   See page 84.

EVAL(´character(s)´)   Returns the numerical value of a string of
                       characters if such a string is a syntacti-
                       cally correct arithmetic expression.

FAIL   Match is guaranteed to fail repeatedly as
                       each alternative is tried; useful with
                       immediate value assignment ($) to see the
                       alternatives tried in a match.

FENCE   Matches nothing; once passed in a left-
                       to-right scan, it creates a barrier or fence
                       so the cursor cannot back up past it in
                       trying alternatives.

FIELD(datatype,n)   Returns the name of the nth field in the
                       user-defined datatype.

GE(x,y)   See page 84.

GT(x,y)   See page 84.

IDENT(variable.1,variable.2)   See page 87.

INPUT(´name´)   Name now does what the use of INPUT did.

INTEGER(´character(s)´)

                            Succeeds if characters

                            are an integer.

ITEM(array.or.table,n)

                            Returns the contents of the nth

                            item or cell of an array or table.

LE(x,y)   See page 84.

LEN(n)   See page 58.

LGT(variable.1,variable.2)   See page 88.

LOAD('function','library')

                            Brings in an external function

                            to the SNOBOL library; installation

                            dependent.

LOCAL(function,n)   Returns the name of the nth local argument

                            of a function.

LT(x,y)   See page 84.

NE(x,y)   See page 84.

NOTANY('character(s)')

                            Matches the first character in

                            a variable that is different from any of the

                            characters in its arguments.

OPSYN('new','old',n) The new and old things are declared synony-

                            mous. If n = 0, the things are understood

to be functions; if n = 1, unary operators;
n = 2, binary operators. (When n equals 1
or 2 and the things are not operators, they
are treated as functions.)

OUTPUT(´name´)   Name now does what OUTPUT did.

POS(n)   Matches nothing and succeeds if the match
                        has proceeded through the nth character from
                        the beginning of the scanned string.

PROTOTYPE(array)   Returns the characters used in defining an
                        array.

REM   See page 62.

REMDR(x,y)   Returns the remainder obtained by dividing
                        the integer x by the integer y.

REPLACE(variable,´abc´,´xyz´)
                        The value returned is the contents of the
                        specified variable with all a´s replaced by
                        x´s, all b´s replaced by y´s, all c´s
                        replaced by z´s, etc. Any two strings can
                        be used for the last two arguments of this
                        function as long as they are the same length
                        because REPLACE() interchanges characters on
                        a one-for-one basis.

REWIND()   Data file handling; installation dependent.

RPOS(n)   Matches nothing and succeeds if the match
                               has proceeded up to the nth character as
                               counted from the end of the scanned string.

RTAB(n)   Matches from the current position up to but
                               not including the nth character counted from
                               the end of the scanned string.

SIZE(variable)   See page 90.

SPAN('character(s)') See page 56.

STOPTR('name','type')

                               Tracing of the given type is stopped for
                               the specified name.

SUCCEED   Acts like a barrier in a match because
                               whenever the cursor is backed into it, it
                               succeeds, hence sending it again in the
                               left-to-right direction.

TAB(n)   Matches from the current position on through
                               the nth character counted from the beginning
                               of the scanned string.

TABLE()   See page 140.

TIME()   Evaluates as the number of milliseconds the
                               program has been running.   (Does not include
                               compilation time.)

UNLOAD(´function´)   Removes and undefines a function from the
                        SNOBOL function library. Releases space to
                        other external functions; installation
                        dependent.

VALUE(´datatype.field.name´)
                        Evaluates as the contents of the specified
                        field.

ADDITIONAL
OPERATORS   OPERATION

^$^   Immediate value assignment; like conditional
                                 value assignment (^.^) except a value is
                                 returned as soon as the previous variable or
                                 pattern matches--the whole match need not
                                 succeed.*

^?operand   Evaluates as success if its operand suc-
                                 ceeds; as failure if it fails.

^~operand   Evaluates as success if its operand fails;
                                 as failure if it succeeds.

^.variable   Evaluates as the name of a created variable
                                 such as the real name for a cell in an array
                                 or table.

^*variable   The literal characters in variable remain
                                 unevaluated until used in a match.

---

*"^" is again being used to indicate the requirement for at least
one space.

APPENDIX 3: Arrays, Tables, and Data Types

ARRAYS. A series of variables which can be referenced in
numerical order is called an array. SNOBOL specifies no intrinsic
limit on the number of dimensions an array may have. A
two-dimensional array with eight rows and eight columns can be
de﹣ined as follows:

        CHECKER.BOARD = ARRAY('8,8')

The cell in the third row, second column in this array is easily
assigned contents:

        CHECKER.BOARD<3,2> = 'RED'

The special symbols < and > are required here; they do not indicate literal contents as they did in Chapter 2. The subscripts
for CHECKER.BOARD<> can be variables as well as literal numbers.
Further it is possible to do arithmetic within the subscript
fields of an array reference:

        OUTPUT = CHECKER.BOARD<R,C + 1>

Given the above assignment, this code would print RED if R equaled
3 and C equaled 1.

TABLES.   A group of variables which is referenced by subscripts
which are NOT NECESSARILY NUMERIC is considered a table.   Using
tables is similar to using indirect reference; in both cases
literal characters (in a variable or not) can be used to indicate
a specific name.   Tables can have only one dimension.   The
following statement defines a table with 100 cells.

```
SALARY = TABLE(100)
```

Using this table is very simple:

```
NAME = 'HAROLD'
SALARY<NAME> = 12000
OUTPUT = '$' SALARY<NAME>
```

This code would print $12000.

USER-DEFINED DATATYPES.   A user can define structures of his
own creation.   A brief example will indcate the potential of this
technique.   Consider a box with two fields:

RECORD

PROBLEMS   POINTS

This structure can be thought of as representing a student's
cumulative accomplishments in a programming course (see sample
program in Appendix 4).   This particular kind of structure has
been called a RECORD.   The name for a SPECIFIC occurrence of this
RECORD could be the student's last name.

This box structure could be manipulated fairly simply. The

datatype RECORD would be defined:

          DATA('RECORD(PROBLEMS,POINTS)')

Note that RECORD is NOT a special term in SNOBOL--but that DATA

is. The datatype could be used as follows:

```
          BROWN = RECORD('PAY,SORT,LABELS,','93.5')
 * ABOVE STATEMENT ASSIGNS THE VARIABLE CALLED BROWN
 * AN INSTANCE OF THE DATATYPE CALLED RECORD AND
 * GIVES EACH OF ITS FIELDS AN INITIAL VALUE.
 * THESE FIELDS ARE EASILY REFERENCED:
          OUTPUT = POINTS(BROWN)
          OUTPUT = PROBLEMS(BROWN)
```

This program would then print:

```
 PAY,SORT,LABELS,
 93.5
```

If one wishes to use a different RECORD for each student (as is

done in the grade recording program in Appendix 4), NAME could be

assigned BROWN or any other name and all references to a student's

records could be done with the above code by substituting $NAME

for BROWN. Students could thereby be processed just by assigning

a new last name to NAME (e.g. NAME = INPUT).

Just as with arrays, SNOBOL specifies no intrinsic limit to the

number of fields which a user-defined datatype can have. However,

a person's own conceptual ability as well as the practical space

considerations in a computer frequently puts some real constraints

on this.

APPENDIX 4:   A Sample SNOBOL Program

The following program maintains student records for a programming course. Each student can choose any number of exercises to
do from an instructor-supplied list. When he completes a program
he turns in the deck which has a comment card (with a * in column
one) that indicates his name and the problem he has chosen. The
instructor punches the grade for the student on the card (the
default value is A) and runs a series of such cards as data for
this program.

As each problem has a different difficulty level (which is read
in as data), the program first multiplies the numeric grade times
this difficulty factor to determine how many points the student
has earned. If a student has done a special project not on the
instructor's list, he indicates on his comment card the difficulty
level he and the instructor have agreed upon.

The student's final grade is determined by where his point
total falls in the grade ranges which also come in as data for the
program. Comments in the program explain various other features
of this example. Special attention should be paid to the use of
the datatype RECORD in this program.

```
1                   &ERRLIMIT = 25
2                   TRACE('ERRTYPE','KEYWORD')
          *
          * &ERRLIMIT AND &ERRTYPE ARE USED TO CATCH BAD CARDS USED
          * BY STUDENTS.  BY ALLOWING &ERRLIMIT TO BE GREATER THAN
          * ZERO, AN ERROR WILL NOT CAUSE TERMINATION; FURTHER,
          * THE TYPE OF ERROR WILL BE NOTED BECAUSE &ERRTYPE IS BEING
          * TRACED.  IN ADDITION, IF AN ERROR DOES OCCUR, THERE ARE
          * SEVERAL CHECK POINTS IN THE PROGRAM THAT NOTE THIS
          * AND SET &DUMP TO 1 THUS REQUESTING A DUMP WHICH WILL
          * AID IN TRACKING DOWN THE ERROR.
          *
3                   &TRIM = 1
4                   DATA('RECORD(PROBLEMS,POINTS)')
5                   STUDENTS = ','
6                   COURSE = INPUT
7                   GRADES = INPUT
8         INITIALIZE.GRADES
9                   A       = INPUT
10                  A.MINUS = INPUT
11                  B.PLUS  = INPUT
12                  B       = INPUT
13                  B.MINUS = INPUT
14                  C.PLUS  = INPUT
15                  C       = INPUT
16                  C.MINUS = INPUT
17                  D.PLUS  = INPUT
18                  D       = INPUT
19                  D.MINUS = INPUT
20        INITIALIZE.PROBLEMS    CARD = INPUT ' '
21                  CARD '*****'      :S(RECORD.GRADES)
22                  CARD BREAK(' ') . PROBLEM ' ' =
23                  PROBLEM = 'P:' PROBLEM
24                  CARD BREAK(' ') . $PROBLEM  :(INITIALIZE.PROBLEMS)
          *
          * FIVE STARS INDICATE THE END OF PROBLEM/DIFFICULTY CARDS &
          * THE BEGINNING OF NAME/PROBLEM(DIFFICULTY)/GRADE CARDS
          * FROM STUDENTS.
          *
25        RECORD.GRADES CARD = INPUT ' ' :F(SPACE.UP)
          *
          * SAMPLE STUDENT INPUT:
          * *   SMITH    22B    3.5  (* IS IN COL. 1; THERE IS VARIABLE
          * SPACING BETWEEN ENTRIES--AT LEAST ONE BLANK IS NECESSARY.)
          *
26                  CARD ('*' SPAN(' ') BREAK(' ') . NAME
26        +         SPAN(' ') BREAK(' ') . PROBLEM) = :F(BAD.CARD)
27                  &DUMP = GT(&ERRTYPE,0) 1
28                  NUM.GRADE = IDENT(CARD,' ') 4 :S(SPECIAL.CHECK)
29                  CARD SPAN(' ') BREAK(' ') . NUM.GRADE
29        +              :S(SPECIAL.CHECK)
30        BAD.CARD   OUTPUT = 'BAD CARD***' CARD :(RECORD.GRADES)
31        SPECIAL.CHECK PROBLEM = 'P:' PROBLEM
32                  PROBLEM '(' (ARB . $PROBLEM) ')'
```

```
33              &DUMP = GT(&ERRTYPE,0) 1
34              STUDENTS ´,´ NAME ´,´         :S(PROBLEM.CHECK)
35              STUDENTS = STUDENTS NAME ´,´
   *
   * AT THIS POINT, NAME CONTAINS THE STUDENT´S NAME,
   * PROBLEM HAS THE PROBLEM CODE, $PROBLEM HAS THE
   * PROBLEM DIFFICULTY, AND NUM.GRADE HAS THE
   * NUMERICAL GRADE (ON A 4 POINT SCALE) AS PUNCHED BY THE
   * INSTRUCTOR.  4 IS ASSUMED IF NO GRADE IS PUNCHED.
   *
   * GET STUDENT´S PAST RECORD--IF ANY.
   *
36              $NAME = RECORD(´ ´,0) :(CREDIT.IT)
37 PROBLEM.CHECK PROBLEMS($NAME) ´ ´ PROBLEM ´ ´
37    +       :S(RECORD.GRADES)
   * ABOVE LINE CHECKS IF STUDENT ALREADY HAS CREDIT
   * FOR THE PROBLEM.
38 CREDIT.IT EXERCISE = PROBLEMS($NAME) PROBLEM ´ ´
39          &DUMP = GT(&ERRTYPE,0) 1
40          TOTAL = POINTS($NAME) + (NUM.GRADE * $PROBLEM) +
40    +          0.000001
41          TOTAL   (BREAK(´.´) ´.´ LEN(3)) . TOTAL
   *
   * UPDATE STUDENT´S RECORD.
   *
42              $NAME = RECORD(EXERCISE,TOTAL)  :(RECORD.GRADES)
43 SPACE.UP      OUTPUT =
44               OUTPUT =
45               OUTPUT =
46              OUTPUT = ´COURSE POINTS AS OF ´ DATE()
46    +                 ´ FOR  ´ COURSE
47               OUTPUT =
48               OUTPUT =
49              STUDENTS ´,´ =
50 SORT         LIST.SAVE = STUDENTS
51              STUDENTS BREAK(´,´) . NAME ´,´ = :F(END)
52 NEXT.NAME STUDENTS BREAK(´,´) . NEW.NAME ´,´ = :F(HAVE.NAME)
53              NAME = LGT(NAME,NEW.NAME) NEW.NAME :(NEXT.NAME)
54 HAVE.NAME STUDENTS = LIST.SAVE
55              STUDENTS NAME ´,´ =
   *
   * DETERMINATION OF LET(TER).GRADE FROM NUM(BER).GRADE.
   *
56      LET.GRADE = GE(POINTS($NAME),A)  ´A´
56    +                :S(COURSE.GRADE)
57      LET.GRADE = GE(POINTS($NAME),A.MINUS) ´A-´
57    +                :S(COURSE.GRADE)
58      LET.GRADE = GE(POINTS($NAME),B.PLUS) ´B+´
58    +                :S(COURSE.GRADE)
59      LET.GRADE = GE(POINTS($NAME),B) ´B´
59    +                :S(COURSE.GRADE)
60      LET.GRADE = GE(POINTS($NAME),B.MINUS) ´B-´
60    +                :S(COURSE.GRADE)
61      LET.GRADE = GE(POINTS($NAME),C.PLUS) ´C+´
```

```
61      +                 :S(COURSE.GRADE)
62          LET.GRADE = GE(POINTS($NAME),C) 'C'
62      +                 :S(COURSE.GRADE)
63          LET.GRADE = GE(POINTS($NAME),C.MINUS) 'C-'
63      +                 :S(COURSE.GRADE)
64          LET.GRADE = GE(POINTS($NAME),D.PLUS) 'D+'
64      +                 :S(COURSE.GRADE)
65          LET.GRADE = GE(POINTS($NAME),D) 'D'
65      +                 :S(COURSE.GRADE)
66          LET.GRADE = GE(POINTS($NAME),D.MINUS) 'D-'
66      +                 :S(COURSE.GRADE)
67          LET.GRADE = 'F'
68      COURSE.GRADE OUTPUT = NAME ' HAS DONE' PROBLEMS($NAME) '.'
69              &DUMP = GT(&ERRTYPE,0) 1
70              OUTPUT = 'WITH ' POINTS($NAME) ' TOTAL POINTS'
71              OUTPUT = IDENT(GRADES,'YES')
71      +             'AND A FINAL GRADE OF ' LET.GRADE
72              OUTPUT =    :(SORT)
73      END
```

COURSE POINTS AS OF 02/21/74 FOR   692: MANG. COMP. FOUNDATION

BARTON HAS DONE P:QUIZ P:23 P:25 P:24 P:16 P:PAPER P:20C P:PAYROLL
(3.0) P:22 P:20I P:EXAM .
WITH 92.559 TOTAL POINTS
AND A FINAL GRADE OF A-

BRONSON HAS DONE P:QUIZ P:SORT P:ADD(2.7) P:23 P:24 P:16 P:25 P:8
P:20A P:PAPER P:PAYROLL(3.0) P:EXAM .
WITH 100.646 TOTAL POINTS
AND A FINAL GRADE OF A

FOGEC HAS DONE P:QUIZ P:PAPER P:ADD(2.7) P:24 P:SORT P:23 P:22 P:G
EN(1.3) P:16 P:EXAM .
WITH 64.085 TOTAL POINTS
AND A FINAL GRADE OF D

LAESER HAS DONE P:QUIZ P:24 P:23 P:16 P:25 P:PAPER P:ADD(2.7) P:SO
RT P:22 P: EXAM .
WITH 86.672 TOTAL POINTS
AND A FINAL GRADE OF B

LUTZ HAS DONE P:16 P:QUIZ P:GROWTH(1.5) P:SORT P:PAPER P:20A P:EXA
M .
WITH 75.000 TOTAL POINTS
AND A FINAL GRADE OF C

MILLER HAS DONE P:22 P:16 P:20A .
WITH 24.875 TOTAL POINTS
AND A FINAL GRADE OF F

NELSON HAS DONE P:16 P:23 P:QUIZ P:ADD(2.7) P:22 P:8 P:SORT P:PAPE
R P:4 P:20A P:EXAM .

WITH 119.621 TOTAL POINTS
AND A FINAL GRADE OF A

RIAN HAS DONE P:QUIZ P:16 P:23 P:24 P:ADD(2.7) P:PAPER P:22 P:SORT
 P:25 P:8 P:EXAM .
WITH 99.924 TOTAL POINTS
AND A FINAL GRADE OF A

SLENTZ HAS DONE P:16 P:QUIZ P:8 P:ADD(2.7) P:SORT P:PAPER P:EXAM .
WITH 66.110 TOTAL POINTS
AND A FINAL GRADE OF D

YUNK HAS DONE P:16 P:QUIZ P:23 P:ADD(2.7) P:22 P:24 P:SORT P:25 P:
PAPER P:20I P:8 P:PAYROLL P:EXAM .
WITH 117.146 TOTAL POINTS
AND A FINAL GRADE OF A

    The following lines were the data for this program:

    692: MANG. COMP. FOUNDATION
    YES
    94
    90
    87
    84
    80
    77
    74
    70
    67
    64
    60
    16 1.5
    22 2.0
    23 1.75
    24 1.3
    25 2
    4 2.3
    8 2.75
    20A 3.5
    20B 3
    20C 2.5
    20D 2.5
    20H 2.5
    20I 2.3
    PAPER 4
    QUIZ 3
    EXAM 5
    ADD 2.5
    SORT 2
    PRICE 2.5
    PAYROLL 2.5

```
PLACEMENT 6
INVENTORY 3.0
*****
*       NELSON   16
*  YUNK   16              3.75
*       NELSON    23        3.5
*  LUTZ    16
*  SLENTZ     16
*      NELSON      QUIZ
*  YUNK   QUIZ                                                    3
*  RIAN  QUIZ                                                     3
*      BRONSON  QUIZ                                              3
   LUTZ   QUIZ                                                    3
*      LAESER     QUIZ                                            2
* BARTON QUIZ                                                     2
       FOGEC     QUIZ                                             2
*   SLENTZ   QUIZ                                                 2
*  YUNK   23
*     NELSON  ADD(2.7)
* BARTON 23                     3.75
*      BRONSON   SORT
*      BRONSON   ADD(2.7)            3.5
*       LAESER              24           3.75
*  YUNK   ADD(2.7)         3.5
*  RIAN   16                    3.75
* SLENTZ 8                      3.75
*  RIAN    23
*     BRONSON 23
*     BRONSON 24
*  SLENTZ   ADD(2.7)
*       LAESER          23
* LUTZ GROWTH(1.5)
* LUTZ SORT
* LUTZ PAPER 3
*  RIAN   24
*      LAESER                 16
*      BRONSON 16
*      BRONSON 25
*  YUNK 22
*      LAESER           25
* SLENTZ SORT                    3.5
*     NELSON 22                      3.75
*  YUNK   24                 3.75
*   SLENTZ   PAPER
*  FOGEC PAPER
*      BRONSON 8
*      BRONSON 20A
*   YUNK   SORT
*  YUNK   25
* BARTON 25
* MILLER 22
* BARTON 24
*      NELSON    8
*      NELSON    SORT
```

```
*     BRONSON PAPER                                                    2.75
*   YUNK  PAPER                                                        3
* BARTON 16                                                           3
*      NELSON    PAPER                                                 3.75
*  MILLER  16          2.5
* RIAN ADD(2.7)               3.0
* BARTON PAPER         3.25
*  RIAN   PAPER            3.75
* MILLER 20A               3.75
* LAESER PAPER 3.25
*      LAESER       ADD(2.7)
*       LAESER     SORT
*        LAESER     22
*  RIAN   22
* RIAN SORT
*     NELSON 4
*     NELSON 20A
*  RIAN   25
*  LUTZ   20A
*  YUNK   20I
*  YUNK   8
* FOGEC ADD(2.7)          3.5
* FOGEC 24                         3.5
* BARTON 20C                       3.5
* BARTON PAYROLL(3.0)              3.5
* BARTON 22                        3.5
* BARTON 20I                       3.5
* FOGEC SORT                       3.5
* FOGEC 23               3.75
*      BRONSON PAYROLL(3.0)
* FOGEC 22
* RIAN 8
*  YUNK   PAYROLL
* FOGEC              GEN(1.3) 3.0
* FOGEC 16 1.75
*     NELSON       EXAM
*  LUTZ  EXAM
* FOGEC   EXAM    0
*       LAESER     EXAM                                              3
*  RIAN   EXAM                                                      3
*  YUNK   EXAM                                                      3
* BARTON EXAM                                                       3
*  SLENTZ   EXAM                                                    2
*     BRONSON EXAM                                                  0
```

APPENDIX 5: FIELDATA Punch Codes for UNIVAC Computers

CHARACTER	ROWS TO BE PUNCHED (IN A GIVEN COLUMN)
:	5 - 8
&	2 - 8
;	11 - 6 - 8
"	11 - 7 - 8 (prints as a smudge)
|	11 - 0 (prints as !)
<	12 - 6 - 8
>	6 - 8
~ (not)	0 - 6 - 8 (prints as _)
?	12 - 0

EXERCISES

1. Write a program which takes a paragraph of text and stores each word in a different cell in a one-dimensional array.

2. Use the array created above and write a program which prints out the stored paragraph at four words per line.

3. Revise the concordance exercise in Chapter 7 so that the list of words is stored as an array or table rather than as a string.

Index